NELSON'S *Quick Guide* TO RELIGIONS

UNDERSTANDING ISLAM

JAMES A. BEVERLEY

THOMAS NELSON PUBLISHERS
Nashville

To
my brother

Bob Beverley

With much love and admiration

Printed in Nashville, Tennessee, by Thomas Nelson, Inc.

Library of Congress Cataloging-in-Publication data is available.

ISBN 0-7852-4897-8

Printed in the United States of America

1 2 3 4 5 — 05 04 03 02 01

Table of Contents

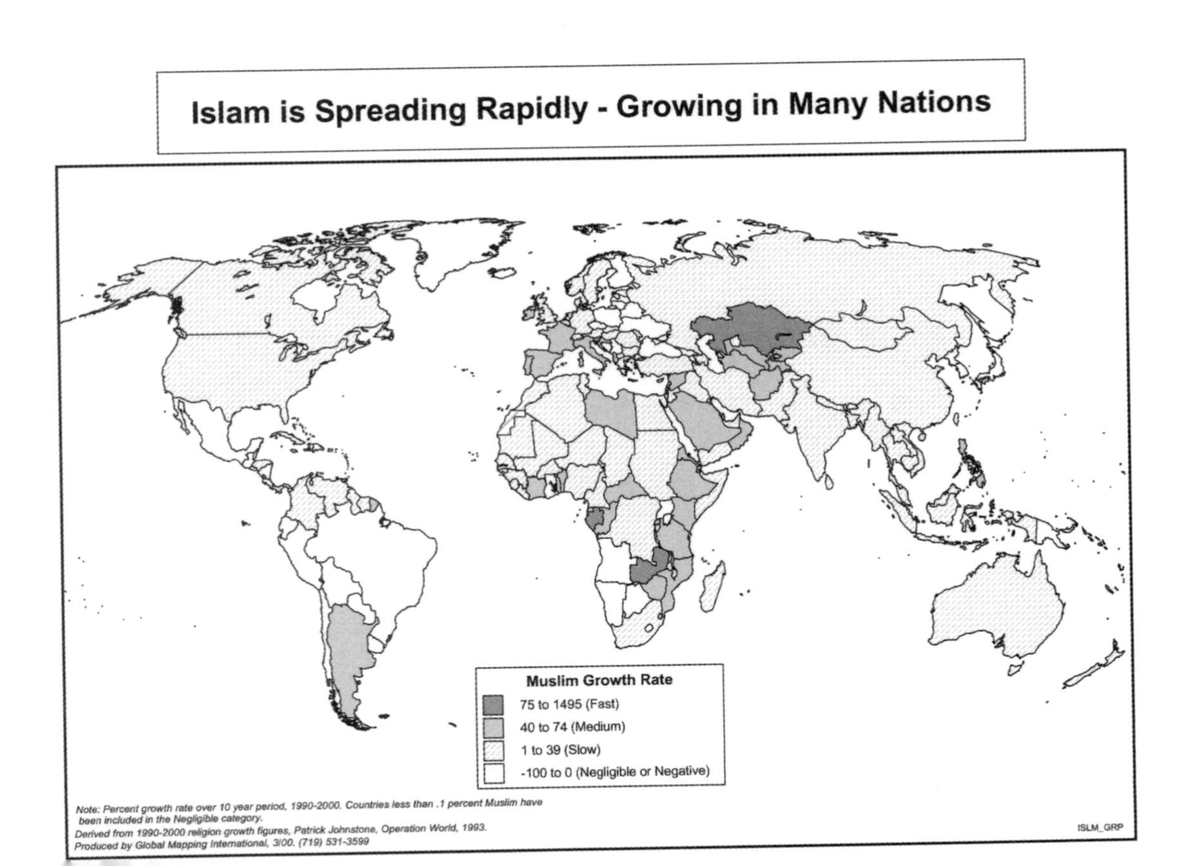
Islam is Spreading Rapidly - Growing in Many Nations
Muslim Growth Rate
75 to 1495 (Fast)
40 to 74 (Medium)
1 to 39 (Slow)
-100 to 0 (Negligible or Negative)
Note: Percent growth rate over 10 year period, 1990-2000. Countries less than .1 percent Muslim have been included in the Negligible category.
Derived from 1990-2000 religion growth figures, Patrick Johnstone, Operation World, 1993.
Produced by Global Mapping International, 3/00. (719) 531-3599
ISLM_GRP

Preface

Most people don't spend a lot of time thinking about religions other than their own. The fact that Islam is the second largest religious movement in the world has been true for many years. Events in the fall of 2001, however, suddenly brought Islam to the attention of people around the world as never before. Who are these people, and what do they really believe? How are they connected to international terrorism?

Muslims in the United States and all over the globe have been placed on the defensive, called upon to explain the basis of their faith. The lack of information about their faith has raised suspicions. Many Muslims have been subjected to verbal and even physical assaults.

Today more than ever before in history there is a need and a demand for information about Islam—about its essential nature, its prophet, and its holy book (the Quran). People want to know what Islam really teaches about the role of women, about *jihad* and terrorism, and about the Palestinian question and their view of Israel. Getting the facts is essential in order for us to keep daily events in perspective.

My aim in this book is to provide accurate, objective, and fair information about all of these issues. *Understanding Islam* is meant to give readers the basic and most important facts and perspectives. Every chapter has been written with attention to the crucial literature and the leading experts on every topic. My aim has been to serve as a reliable and trustworthy guide to momentous and complex topics.

Though I am not a Muslim, I have made every effort to be fair to the Islamic faith, as well as attentive to the critical issues that are being raised about Islam. What I have written is based on years of research as a scholar of world religions. My understanding of Islam is rooted in face-to-face encounters with Muslims in the U.S.A., Canada, India, Kenya, South Africa, and England. My knowledge and perspective is also rooted in learning from friends and colleagues who have spent years living in Muslim countries and under Islamic rule.

In a world in which each day raises new questions, this book seeks to provide some foundational answers. It is hoped that out of an enhanced understanding will come a greater ability to view events from a broader perspective. Since my presentation involves some controversial issues, I ask that my readers examine my book with patience and care. I will give serious attention to thoughtful criticisms.

I am grateful to my wife Gloria, our children, Derek and Andrea, and to our son-in-law Julien for their encouragement. Thanks to Annie McKeown and Rachel Collins for research assistance, and to Kevin Rische and Aaron Matthews for computer help. For comments on argument and perspective, I am grateful to Bob Beverley, Jay Smith, John Wilkinson, Larry Matthews, Donald Wiebe, Bob Morris, J. Gordon Melton, and Mitchell Bard. Thanks also to Wayne Kinde, Lee Hollaway, Teri Wilhelms, Barbara West, and Phil Stoner at Thomas Nelson.

James A. Beverley
jbeverley@tyndale.ca
October 22, 2001

CHAPTER ONE

Islam

The Nature of Islam

One out of every six people on earth is Muslim, a follower of Islam, the second largest religion in the world, next to Christianity. Islam has been a religious, cultural, and political force since the sixth century A.D. Today it plays a dominant role in the Middle East and large sections of Africa and Asia.

The Four Foundations of Islam

As in all religions, Islam has a core, an essence, a sort of DNA that has defined the religion from the beginning. The best way to begin to grasp this basic and fundamental identity is to recognize four absolutely key realities in the faith of all Muslims. Even if you knew everything there was to know about Islam, these keys to understanding the Muslim faith would be the same.

1. What is absolutely primary in Islam is **a total belief in Allah** (the Arabic term for God). Muslims believe with conviction that there is one supreme creator, an infinite, eternal power who can do all things and knows all things.

According to Muslims, Allah is the perfect, wise, merciful, and just Guide who holds all humans accountable for their deeds, both good and bad. All of this is captured in the first verses of the Quran (Koran is the former English term), the primary Muslim scripture. "In the name of Allah, Most Gracious, Most Merciful. Praise be to Allah, the Cherisher and Sustainer of the worlds." It continues: "Master of the Day of Judgment. You do we worship, and Your aid we seek. Show us the straight way."

2. Muslims also believe that Allah has spoken to the world through **Muhammad, the final and greatest Prophet.** The vast majority of Muslims believe that Muhammad (who died in A.D. 632) was sinless. Every area of Islamic life is patterned after what Muhammad taught, what he did, how he dressed, how he responded to threats, and what he said had been revealed to him by Allah.

The reverence and adulation of Muhammad is hard to overstate, though Muslims do not believe he was divine. However, those who cast aspersions on the prophet are in extreme danger, as Salman Rushdie, the Indian-born Muslim, discovered when he wrote *The Satanic Verses*. The Iranian Ayatollah Khomeini issued a death order on him because he thought Rushdie had slandered Muhammad.

3. Further, **the Quran is absolutely fundamental** to all Muslims. This is *the* Holy Book. Muslims believe the Quran was revealed to Muhammad and is the literal, actual Word of Allah. It should be recited in Arabic, the original language, and memorized, studied, but never questioned.

Islamic views on everything are determined by what the Quran says or by what can be deduced from its general teachings. Thus, polygamy is acceptable because the Quran says so. Muslim veiling of women is derived from one passage that demands modesty. The hand of a thief is amputated simply because the Quran says this is to be the punishment. Muslims have certain views about Jesus because the Muslim holy book teaches so.

4. Islam is also **a religion of law.** While every religion has general principles, some religions like Orthodox Judaism and Roman Catholicism have elaborate rules and regulations. This is even more so in Islam, since Islamic law extends to every area of life, including how Muslim nations are to obey God's will, known as *Shariah* [SHAR rih ah].

The history of Islamic jurisprudence is very long and complicated, especially after Islam experienced a serious division following the death of Muhammad. Basically, however, Islamic law is derived first from the Quran, and then from the example (*sunnah*) of Muhammad. When neither the Quran nor the Prophet's life and teachings speak directly on issues, most Muslim legal authorities depend on reason and consensus to formulate either new laws or judgments based on the massive codes of law given in the three centuries after Muhammad's death.

The scope of *shariah* law is amazing to most non-Muslims. Consider, for example, some of the matters addressed in *Islamic Laws,* written by Ayatullah al Uzama Sye Ali-al-Husaini Seestani, a famous judge in Iran. He provides rulings (known as *fatwas*) on thousands of topics, including: (a) what direction should be faced when using the bathroom, (b) when swallowing thick dust makes fasting void, and (c) how much is owed Allah in alms-giving if a Muslim owns 61 camels.

The Five Pillars of Islam

Just as the Ten Commandments shape Judaism, the five pillars of Islam constitute core patterns of faith for most Muslims who have ever lived.

- **Confession.** The primary pillar is a confession of faith known as the *shahadah,* which reads: "There is no God but Allah, and Muhammad is His messenger." Devout Muslims repeat this statement several times each day.
- **Prayer.** The second pillar involves the discipline of prayer (*salat*) and the call to all Muslims to pray at five specific times every day, facing Mecca, the holiest city. In traditional Islamic cultures, the call to prayer, resounding from the *minarets* (towers) of the *mosques* (temples), brings all other activity to a halt.
- **Giving.** This third pillar is known as *zakat*. The *zakat* is collected by a few Muslim states but most Muslims give through leaving money in the metal *zakat* box in their local mosque. The money is used to help the poor and for emergency situations. The *zakat* involves giving 2.5% of the Muslim's assets but is not charity since it is an obligatory act, one that is usually to be done in private.
- **Fasting.** Muslims are to intensify their spiritual focus through the fourth pillar *sawm* (fasting), from sun-up to sundown during the entire month of Ramadan (the ninth month in the Islamic calendar). Unless prohibited by bad health, all Muslims are to abstain from all food, water, and sexual activity from sunrise to sunset during the month of Ramadan. The fast offers a time for spiritual reflection, repentance, and giving to the poor. The whole Quran is often recited in evening worship over the thirty-day period. Ramadan ends with a three-day feast.
- **Pilgrimage.** The fifth pillar, known as the *hajj,* is the command for all able-bodied Muslims to make a

pilgrimage to Mecca at least once in their lifetime. Every year two million Muslim pilgrims make their way to Mecca. Outside the city both males and females don simple white garments, and enter Mecca while reciting "Here I am at your service, O God, here I am!" They circle seven times around the Kaba, the temple built by Abraham and Ishma'il. The pilgrims engage in a ritual of running between two mountains outside of Mecca, in memory of the plight of Hagar looking for food and water. Muslims also throw stones at a pillar that symbolizes Satan, and sacrifice animals in memory of the story of Abraham and Isaac.

Seven Other Major Beliefs

From the above, we know that all faithful Muslims believe that Allah is the one true God. They also want to emulate Muhammad, obey the Quran, pray, give financially, fast, take the pilgrim's journey to Mecca, and obey the law of God in all things. Beyond these over-riding and paramount aspects of Islam, seven other fundamental beliefs help paint an accurate picture.

1. **Muslims believe that Islam began long before Muhammad. They assert that Islam started when God created Adam and Eve, and that Islam was the religion of faithful Jews and Christians.** Thus, Jews in the time of Moses were Muslims, and Christians in the time of Jesus were Muslims! Younis Shaikh, who taught at a medical college in Pakistan, was arrested in October 2000 for allegedly saying that Muhammad's parents were not Muslims and that Muhammad did not become a Muslim until he was 40.

2. Though Muslim views are similar in some ways to Christian tradition, **Muslims do not believe in original sin.** This is the concept that all human beings are born with a sinful nature. Muslims do believe that Adam rebelled against God's law in the Garden of Eden, but there was no fall of the human race, as is taught by most Christian groups. Humans are frail and weak, prone to temptation, obviously, but not predisposed toward sin.

3. **Muslims believe in the total sovereignty of God.** Islam's emphasis on this belief cannot be overstressed. In parts of Afghanistan, goals in soccer games are celebrated by shouting "Allahu Akbar" or "God is great." When I visited Kenya in 1994, I saw a vivid display of Islamic trust in God as I visited a poor Muslim area. There, on top of the most pitiful little "house" you can imagine, the "home owner" had a sign, bigger than his house, proclaiming his faith in the great Allah.

Muslim theologians developed a very rigid doctrine of predestination out of the emphasis on Allah's total supremacy. If God is all-knowing and all-powerful, He must, in some sense, be responsible for everything. If nothing really deviates from His will, and He knows the future, everything must be predestined—or so it has been argued. Some analysts of Muslim culture believe that a sense of fatalism has emerged as a result of this Islamic preoccupation with predestination.

4. **Islam also teaches that our universe is home to angels, devils, and another kind of spirit beings known as *jinns*.** Islam shares with Christian tradition a belief in Satan or the supreme devil, an angel who chose to rebel against Allah. Muslims also believe in angels, disembodied spirits who obey God. The English term "genie"

derives from Muslim stories about the *jinn,* supernatural entities who can do both good and evil.

5. **Islam has very definite views about the Day of Judgment.** At a time known only to Allah, the world will end. All humans will be judged by their deeds. Humans await either eternal punishment in hell fire or eternal bliss in heaven. Islam has no Catholic notion of purgatory, and virtually no openness to any idea that all humans will eventually reach paradise.

The explicitness of Islam on the severity of hell fire makes frightening reading. One famous verse in the fourth *surah* (chapter) of the Quran states: "Those who reject our Signs, We shall soon cast into the Fire: as often as their skins are roasted through, We shall change them for fresh skins, that they may taste the penalty: for God is Exalted in Power, Wise." (v. 56)

6. **Muslims believe that heaven is the eternal home of the righteous.** It is described in the Quran as a wonderful garden paradise, an image especially appealing to Muslims used to the sands of the Arabian deserts. There will be no sin, no death, and no tears in heaven. There will be special reward for Muslim martyrs. Some traditions imply that no Jews or Christians will be in heaven, only Muslims. A few famous verses in the Quran promise that faithful Muslim men will be rewarded by beautiful women when they enter paradise. For both men and women the Quran states that "the greatest bliss is the good pleasure of Allah." (9:72)

7. **Muslims claim that Jesus is a prophet of Islam.** Given the bitter hostilities between Islamic and Christian empires in history, it is often assumed that Muslims have no interest in Jesus. While Muhammad is the chief

prophet, Muslims also look to Jesus as a spiritual guide. Often when Muslims speak of Jesus, they will add the phrase "Peace Be Upon Him"—just as they do when Muhammad's name is mentioned either vocally or in print. For short, in writing you will often see "Muhammad (PBUH)" or "Jesus (PBUH)".

There are significant differences between Muslim and Christian understandings of Jesus. This is most easily seen by a list of Muslim negative assertions about Christian views. For Islam, Jesus is not the Son of God and not an incarnation of God. Jesus is not divine. He did not die on the Cross at Calvary. His death is not a sacrifice for sin. He was not put in a tomb outside Jerusalem. The Christian story of Easter is not true, though Muslims do believe that Jesus went to heaven when He died years after attempts to have Him crucified failed.

Muslims do agree with Christianity on the following points: Jesus was born of the Virgin Mary, was a prophet of God, lived a holy life, taught with wisdom and love, and performed many miracles. Muslims also unite with Christian tradition in teaching that Jesus was persecuted for His faith, was opposed to idol worship (as most Jews would be), and is now in heaven.

CHAPTER TWO

Muhammad

Muhammad: the Prophet of Islam

Most secular historians clearly have no interest in following Muhammad, yet some of them regard him as the most significant person in human history. Though Christianity claims more believers, Muhammad is viewed by these historians as having a greater impact on history, given the breadth of Islamic political power, the depth and range of Islamic spirituality, and the pervasive way in which Islam brings its ideology to bear on every facet of life.

Whatever the merit of this judgment, anyone who reviews the history of the world since the seventh century can see the profound impact Muhammad made in his lifetime and since. Muslims believe, of course, that Muhammad is *the* Prophet, the final Messenger of Allah. Thus our understanding of Islam is intrinsically linked with our knowledge and assessment of its Prophet.

The Profile of a Prophet's Life

This profile is based on what most Muslims believe about Muhammad. Many scholars argue that the data about him comes too long after he died to provide historical certainty about his life. Muslims generally accept that he was born about A.D. 570. His was the world of tribal Arabia, where people believed in many gods.

Muhammad knew pain early in his life. By age six or so he had lost both parents, first his mother just after he

Muhammad's Life at a Glance

c. A.D. 570	Birth in Mecca
595	Marriage to Khadijah, a travel merchant
610	Claims to have divine revelations through mystical experience
613	Begins to preach monotheistic message and endures persecution
619	After the death of Khadijah, Muhammad marries Sawdah, first of many other wives.
620	Angel Gabriel takes Muhammad to Jerusalem and he ascends to seventh heaven on a ladder
622	Escape to Medina to avoid persecution in Mecca
624	Muhammad defeats Meccan enemies at the battle of Badr
630	Muhammad conquers his enemies at Mecca and removes idols from city
632	Muhammad dies on June 8 after a period of ill health

was born, and later his father. His grandfather raised him for two years and then his grandfather died. An uncle then took care of him until Muhammad reached his teen years. Some scholars of religion speculate on how these early losses may have impacted him personally in terms of his later ideology and behavior.

A woman merchant named Khadijah came into Muhammad's life and they were married in 595, when Muhammad was about 25. Though she was considerably older, she bore him at least six children, and by all indications they had a loving marriage. Muhammad did not have other wives until after Khadijah's death in 619.

Muhammad's life changed forever in the year 610, on the seventeenth night of the Arabic month Ramadan. Muhammad claimed that the angel Gabriel visited him on Mount Hira, near Mecca, in a powerful, terrifying, and transforming encounter. According to the earliest documents, Muhammad returned home, shaken by this encounter, and turned to his wife for confirmation of his prophetic call.

Three years later Muhammad began to preach to his Meccan neighbors. His message of one God met fierce resistance. Arabs were polytheistic and Mecca's main shrine, the Kaba, said to be built by Abraham, was home to many gods. Muhammad gained some converts immediately, one of the most famous being his friend Abu Bakr. His earliest followers came mainly from the poor clans of Mecca, drawn to Muhammad's message of social reform.

Muslims believe that in 620, one year after the death of Muhammad's first wife, the angel Gabriel brought Muhammad by night to Jerusalem on the back of a heavenly horse named Buruq. In the holy city the prophet conversed with Jesus, Moses, and Abraham. Then, according to the Quran, Muhammad and his angel companion were taken by ladder to the seventh heaven. Muslims believe that the Dome of the Rock in Jerusalem is built on the spot from which Muhammad ascended. This episode is known as the *miraj*.

Two years later, in 622, in year one of the Muslim calendar, Muhammad was forced to flee to Medina, about 250 miles north of Mecca. Then, for eight long and bitter years, the Prophet engaged in repeated military battles with his Meccan enemies. There were significant victories (most notably on March 15, 624, at Badr) and major setbacks, one being at Uhud just a year later.

By January 630, however, Muhammad triumphed, took control of Mecca, and destroyed the idols in the Kaba. Medina continued to be his home base. He led military campaigns in northern Arabia, and returned to Mecca for a final pilgrimage in early 632. He was in poor health at the time, traveled back to Medina, and died on June 8 of that year, in the embrace of Aisha, one of his many wives.

Alfred North Whitehead once said that "philosophy is one long footnote to Plato." Likewise, Islamic history is one long footnote to Muhammad. Thus, Muhammad's journey—in all of its detail, from the mode of his prayer life, to his treatment of Jews and Christians, to what he did in battle—becomes the example for all Muslims.

Muhammad's life must not be compartmentalized, as if his spiritual life was distinct from his family life, or military career, or political strategies, or economic views. For Muhammad, and for Muslims generally, they are part of a seamless whole. Islam continues this pattern by refusing to think that the religious and the secular should be divorced. Thus, most Muslims would have no respect for the American model of the "separation of church and state."

Historical Accuracy and Muhammad

As we will see in the next section, there is a wide range of opinion about Muhammad. Part of that difference arises out of varied estimates about how certain we can be historically about his life. There are five major sources for historical analysis: (1) the Quran, (2) biographies of the prophet, (3) *hadith* (sayings of Muhammad), (4) *tafsir* (commentaries), and (5) *ta'rikh* (Muslim histories).

Of these, the study of the *hadith* represents one of the most fascinating aspects of Islamic history and religious life. Muslim scholars had to try and sort through the hundreds of thousands of traditions about Muhammad in order to decide what reports were accurate. The most famous collection of what Muslims regard as authentic *hadith* was done by al-Bukhari (d. 870).

Western scholars have been divided over the value of the *hadith* in terms of what we can know about Muhammad. The traditions obviously tell us what Muslims and others were saying about the Prophet, and that has an interest for its own sake. There is increasing skepticism among experts about the value of both the Quran and *hadith* in giving us trustworthy data on Muhammad.

Of course, there remains an immense gap between Muslim scholars who accept everything from the Quran and the *hadith* and those non-Muslim historians who feel it is their responsibility to judge the historical integrity of both—to judge both at other levels as well. Thus, a Western academic may accept a particular saying or deed of Muhammad as historical but use that teaching or action as evidence that Muhammad is not the prophet of God.

Three Basic Views of Muhammad

That there is an extreme range in opinion about Muhammad should come as no surprise, given the radical divergence about him in his lifetime, and given the incredible things said for him and against him down through the centuries. Many wars have been fought over his ideology, even among Muslims. In the Iran-Iraq conflict in the early 1980s, where millions died, both countries claimed to have Muhammad on their side, much like Irish Catholics and Protestants assert that Jesus is with them when they fight each other. Three distinct views cover the range of interpretation about the prophet.

1. Of first significance is the faithful Muslim understanding of Muhammad, mentioned briefly in the opening chapter, but deserving of greater attention. The adulation of Muhammad by Muslims parallels the Christian adoration of Jesus, the Hindu love for Krishna, the Sikh reverence for Guru Nanak, and the Buddhist focus on Gautama Buddha.

Consider these words from a Muslim writer of the Middle Ages: "When cutting your nails you must begin with the little toe of the right foot and finish with the little toe of the left foot." This is from al-Ghazali, one of Islam's greatest thinkers, a figure recognized by all historians of philosophy. Al-Ghazali tells how toenails should be cut for one simple reason: this is how the Prophet did it.

Out of this immense adulation of Muhammad comes an equal anger against any who are perceived as ridiculing the Prophet. For example, Ahmed Deedat, one of the most popular defenders of Islam, circulated a pamphlet against the novelist Salman Rushdie, called *How Rushdie Fooled the West.* His conclusion about Rushdie speaks for itself: "Mired in misery, may all his filthy lucre choke in his throat, and may he die a coward's death, a hundred times a day, and eventually when death catches up with him, may he simmer in hell for all eternity!"

Miracle Stories About Muhammad

1. The Quran as perfect book proves Allah as author
2. Taken on supernatural trip to Jerusalem and heaven
3. Prophet splits the moon in two to prove Islam
4. Angel opens Prophet's chest and washes his heart
5. Prophet multiplies food to feed hungry disciples
6. Water supply flows through Prophet's fingers
7. Wolf praises Muhammad's ministry
8. Muhammad heals crying palm tree
9. 3,000 angels help Muhammad in battle
10. Two trees move to provide privacy for Prophet

2. A second assessment of Muhammad is one step removed from Islamic orthodoxy, though a major step. We move to those who have a high opinion of Muhammad but do not accept, for various reasons, that he is *the* prophet of God, or that Islam is the one true religion. Thus, Alphonse de LaMartaine, writing in a history of the Turks, said:

> If greatness of purpose, smallness of means, and astonishing results are the three criteria of a human genius, who could dare compare any great man in history with Muhammad? The most famous men created arms, laws, and empires only. They founded, if anything at all, no more than material powers which often crumbled away before their eyes. This man moved not only armies, legislations, empires, peoples, dynasties, but millions of men in one-third of the then inhabited world; and more than that, he moved the altars, the gods, the religions, the ideas, the beliefs and the souls.

Hans Küng, a Roman Catholic, took up the question of Muhammad's status in his book *Christianity and the World Religions*. He presents seven parallels between Muhammad and the prophets of Israel, outlines the immense contribution of Muhammad, and concludes by citing Vatican II, where one of the documents states that the Catholic Church "also looks upon the Muslims with great respect: They worship the one true God who has spoken to man."

Küng, who does not believe that Muhammad was sinless or that Islam is the one true religion, then offers this assessment: "In my opinion, that Church—and all the Christian Churches—must also 'look with great respect' upon the man whose name is omitted from the declaration out of embarrassment, although he alone led the Muslims to the worship of the one God, who spoke *through* him: Muhammad the Prophet."

3. The third view moves to a whole other realm, one in which Muhammad becomes the embodiment of evil. This tradition of contempt began in the early Middle Ages as Christian and Muslim armies fought from North Africa, across the Middle East, and into Europe. Many Christians, popes included, viewed the wars as the necessary struggle against the Antichrist himself—Muhammad.

Dante's *Inferno* puts the Islamic leader in the lower realms of hell. William E. Phipps, author of *Muhammad and Jesus,* describes Dante's vision of Muhammad's fate. "There he receives everlastingly some of the worse punishment that hell has to offer. A gash from throat to anus causes his intestines to hang between his legs. Many of the damned are so so horrified by the mutilated Muhammad spectacle that they forget momentarily their own torment."

Such diatribes against Muhammad continue from Dante through the Reformation period, culminating in Luther's invective, quoted by Phipps: "Should you be called a prophet, who were such an uncouth blockhead and ass? When the spirit of lies had taken possession of Muhammad, and the devil had murdered men's souls with his Quran and had destroyed the faith of Christians, he had to go on and take the sword and set about to murder their bodies."

Secular writers have dismissed Muhammad with less contempt, but their views follow the same pattern: Muhammad was ignorant, barbaric, and immoral. He was either a hypocrite or delusional, perhaps the victim of epileptic seizures, whose success with converts has more to do with promises of sexual reward, material gain, and the proverbial Islamic sword.

In the aftermath of September 11, 2001, some editorials in the secular press hinted at Muhammad's dark side, with subtle accusations that the terror that rained down on New York and Washington has its roots in the life and teaching of the Muslim prophet. They cite Muhammad's all-or-nothing mentality, his expansionist vision, his dictatorship, and, of course, his love for *Jihad*.

One interesting factor here is that human beings arrive at radically different views while dealing with the same person, the same documents, and the same history. One author finds Muhammad racist, lustful, and irrational. He argues that his views are based on a careful reading of the *hadith* material about Muhammad. Muslims read the same traditions and regard them as proof that Muhammad was sinless and the greatest person who has ever lived.

If we look at a particular issue in *hadith* interpretation, we discover that the debate is not usually over what this or that tradition states. Muslim scholars know very well what particular *hadith* is being used to justify each specific attack on Muhammad. The difference of opinion has to do with larger philosophical, religious, and psychological views that are brought to the given issue.

Take, for instance, the incredible accusation that Muhammad was a pedophile. It is hard to imagine a more explosive thing to say about a religious leader, or anyone for that matter. Some Muslim scholars may want this accuser to die, but they know that he is referring to an infamous episode in the prophet's life when he took a very young girl to be his wife.

How could any Muslim scholar defend this today? First, some would simply refuse to entertain any possibility that Muhammad could sin. "He is the Prophet (Peace Be Upon Him), he is sinless. I cannot question God's Apostle (Peace Be Upon Him)." A second tactic would be to explain the event by reference to different cultural norms in Muhammad's day. "Who are we to judge another culture and their norms in marriage and family life?"

Finally, other Muslim scholars might say that the Prophet is exempt from the moral standards that apply to normal humans. "Allah, the Sovereign Lord, alone decides what is right. His ways are beyond our understanding. We must trust him no matter what. Allah, in his infinite wisdom, gave the young bride to Muhammad (Peace Be Upon Him). Allah knows what is best."

A more likely process is for Muslims to resist all accusations against Muhammad by a reflex action that finds refuge in the sacred and eternal truths given by Allah through His Prophet. The thought that these truths can be shaken is simply beyond the imagination of most Muslims. Then, out of this faith and certainty, comes the challenge to all non-Muslims to read the Quran and see for themselves that God has given His Word in miraculous form to a weary and skeptical world.

When Muhammad was alive, he met challenges about his credibility by pointing to the amazing revelation that had been given to him from God's angel. To Muslims, that book proves the truth of Islam. That book is the focus of our next chapter.

CHAPTER THREE

Quran

The Quran: the Muslim Holy Book

Yusaf Ali's English translation of the Quran runs to 597 pages in one paperback edition. That is one indication of the space taken up by the Quran's 6,000 or so verses. There is nothing amazing about the size of the Quran. What is amazing is that many Muslims, including young boys and girls, have memorized the entire Quran, cover to cover, in Arabic.

This remarkable feat is an indication of the incredible stature of the Quran within the Muslim world. It is a sin for a Muslim to place any book or object on top of the Quran. Every debate in Islamic law is settled by what the Quran teaches. Muslim scholars who have condemned the September 11, 2001 terrorist attack have done so on the basis of their belief that the Quran condemns such evil.

The Origin of the Quran

Muslims believe that the **origin of the Quran lies with Allah** (85:22). Then, when the time was right, according to the will of Allah, the angel Gabriel dictated the revelations to Muhammad. He recited the words to his wife and then to the small group that became his first followers. The earliest members not only memorized the unfolding contents but also started to write them down. After Muhammad died, a number of Muslim scholars formed the final edition of the Quran.

Most Muslims absolutely reject theories about its alleged human origins. Islam states quite plainly that the Quran has one author: Allah. It is not Muhammad's book. It is not, they say, a human book. It is divine. To question the Quran is to risk eternal punishment. To obey it is to gain eternal life.

Many scholars believe that the Quran lacks historical reliability since it cannot be traced back to Muhammad. Muslims believe that the Quran is perfect and contains no errors. What Allah revealed to Muhammad was passed on faithfully by the Prophet, according to Muslim tradition, with one famous and startling exception. Early in his work as a prophet, Satan fooled Muhammad into thinking that true followers of Allah could worship three Arab deities. For a very brief period, one of the chapters of the Quran contained approval of such pagan worship.

As soon as Allah told Muhammad of the deception by Satan, the Prophet moved quickly to remove the offending passage. Ever since, these verses have been called "the Satanic verses." This episode in the life of the Prophet is mentioned in the Quran, in the *hadith* or traditions about the Prophet, and in countless books. It is from this incident that Salman Rushdie titled his controversial novel.

The Structure of the Quran

The Quran contains 114 *surahs* or chapters, and over 6,000 verses. The surahs are arranged by size, with the shorter chapters near the end. It is generally believed that the later chapters were written first and belong to the period when the Prophet was in Medina. The longer chapters were written last and were revealed after the Prophet conquered Mecca.

The titles of the various chapters are based on some word or idea that appears in the chapter, though the titles do not usually suggest what is the main theme of the chapter, if there is one. Some Muslim scholars teach that there are hidden scientific truths and hidden mathematical wonders in the Quran. For example, one writer argues that the divine inspiration of the Quran is proven by the fact that the Arabic word for "Most Merciful" is used 114 times, which matches exactly the number of surahs of the Quran.

The Eight Major Themes of the Quran

Many first time readers of the Quran find it confusing. It does not seem orderly, as most Muslims will acknowledge. The text does not follow a narrative, and it is not written in a systematic fashion. The surahs are not arranged by content, and there is no single theme in most chapters. The best way to understand the Quran is to first grasp the major themes that it addresses on its pages.

1. **Allah.** The Quran is absolutely dominated by reference to God. Verse after verse, page after page, beginning to end, Allah is everything to the Quran. The word Allah appears over 2,500 times. Anyone who says that the Quran is mainly about something else has never read the Quran. It is a book saturated with references to God. Here are ten major things, in alphabetical order, that the Quran says about Allah.

- **He is the Creator.** Surah 6:101–102 states: "He created all things, and He hath full knowledge of all things. That is God, your Lord! there is no god but He, the Creator of all things." Another passage expresses it this way. "He is God, the Creator, the Evolver, the Bestower of Forms (or Colors). To Him belong the Most Beautiful Names: whatever is in the heavens and on earth, doth declare His Praises and Glory: and He is the Exalted in Might, the Wise." (59:24)

- **He is Eternal.** "God! There is no god but He, the Living, the Self-subsisting, Eternal. No slumber can seize Him nor sleep." (2:225) Verse two of Surah 3 states: "God! There is no god but He—the Living, the Self-Subsisting, Eternal." In the 112th Surah, it simply says: "God, the Eternal, Absolute." (v. 2)
- **He is the Guardian.** In Surah 89:14, near the end of the Quran, we read: "For thy Lord is (as a Guardian) on a watch-tower." An earlier surah reads: "O mankind! reverence your Guardian-Lord, who created you from a single person, created, of like nature, His mate, and from them twain scattered (like seeds) countless men and women—reverence God, through whom ye demand your mutual (rights), and (reverence) the wombs (that bore you): for God ever watches over you." (4:1)
- **He is Holy.** "Whatever is in the heavens and on earth, doth declare the Praises and Glory of God—the Sovereign, the Holy One, the Exalted in Might, the Wise." (62:1) God's holiness is also expressed in His goodness, as in 3:26: "In Thy hand is all good." Later, in the same surah, we read: "God loves those who do good." (v. 134)
- **He is the all-Knowing.** Surah 35:38 speaks of the scope of God's knowledge. "Verily God knows (all) the hidden things of the heavens and the earth: verily He has

full knowledge of all that is in (men's) hearts." An earlier surah also reads: "He knows all that goes into the earth, and all that comes out thereof; all that comes down from the sky and all that ascends thereto."

- **He is the Lord of All.** "And do ye join equals with Him? He is the Lord of (all) the Worlds." (41:9) This theme is also expressed in terms of God's sovereignty, as in these powerful words from Surah 59:23: "God is He, than Whom there is no other god—the Sovereign, the Holy One, the Source of Peace (and Perfection), the Guardian of Faith, the Preserver of Safety, the Exalted in Might, the Irresistible, the Supreme: Glory to God!"
- **He is Merciful.** "He is the Most Merciful of those who show mercy!" (12:64) The phrase "Oft-forgiving, Most Merciful" is used over and over again in the Quran, six times just in Surah 9 alone. Another powerful expression of God's mercy is given in an earlier surah: "Those who believed and those who suffered exile and fought (and strove and struggled) in the path of God,—they have the hope of the Mercy of God: And God is Oft-forgiving, Most Merciful."
- **He is the Revealer.** The Quran longs for people to trust in God's revelation and expresses astonishment that humans ignore what Allah has shown them. "If only they had stood fast by the Law, the Gospel, and all the revelation that was sent to them from their Lord, they would have enjoyed happiness from every side." (5:56) In Surah 3 we find a celebration of Jews and Christians who follow Allah's revelation: "And there are, certainly, among the People of the Book, those who believe in God, in the revelation to you,

and in the revelation to them, bowing in humility to God: They will not sell the Signs of God for a miserable gain! For them is a reward with their Lord." (v. 199

- **He is the Sustainer.** One of the more beautiful passages is Surah 7:54, which reads: "Your Guardian-Lord is God, Who created the heavens and the earth in six days, and is firmly established on the throne (of authority): He draweth the night as a veil o'er the day, each seeking the other in rapid succession: He created the sun, the moon, and the stars, (all) governed by laws under His command. Is it not His to create and to govern? Blessed be God, the Cherisher and Sustainer of the worlds!"
- **He is worthy of worship.** This is expressed by stating repeatedly that God is worthy of praise. God himself commands worship, as in 20:14: "Verily, I am God: There is no god but I: So serve thou Me (only), and establish regular prayer for celebrating My praise."

2. **Muhammad.** The prophet himself is at the center of the Quran, though often as a figure behind every chapter. His name is mentioned only four times, but he is the subject of many passages. Muslims do not believe that Muhammad is writing about himself, however. Islam teaches that Gabriel dictated to Muhammad material that was to be put in the Quran about Muhammad! Further, when the Quran quotes words from Muhammad, Muslims believe that these are words that Allah tells Muhammad to say.

Muhammad has, according to the Quran, an incredible status because Allah called him as a prophet. In fact, he is "the Seal of the Prophets," a phrase from the famous passage in Surah 33 that is used by Muslims to argue that Muhammad is the final prophet. In addition, Muhammad is a judge to his followers (4:65), and is to be respected by them (2:104; 4:46).

Allah himself is a witness to Muhammad's mission (13:43; and 46:8). Further, the Quran teaches that Muhammad's prophetic work was predicted by both Moses (46:10) and by Jesus, of whom the Quran says: "And remember, Jesus, the son of Mary, said: 'O Children of Israel! I am the apostle of God (sent) to you, confirming the Law (which came) before me, and giving Glad Tidings of an Apostle to come after me, whose name shall be Ahmad.'" Ahmad is a shortened form of Muhammad.

Muhammad is the universal messenger from God (34:28), the symbol of Allah's mercy to the world (9:61; 28:46–47; 76:24–26), and inspired by Allah. In Surah 53:10–12 it says: "So did (God) convey the inspiration to His Servant—(conveyed) what He (meant) to convey. The (Prophet's) (mind and) heart in no way falsified that which he saw. Will ye then dispute with him concerning what he saw?"

The Quran describes Muhammad as gentle (3:159), very concerned about his followers (9:128), and in deep distress for unbelievers (12:97; 25:30). It says he was a man of prayer (74:3), and had an "exalted standard of character." (68:4) He was often mocked by his enemies in Mecca, and he was accused of being mad (7:184) and under the power of demons (81:22).

Muhammad is told to adore Allah (96:19), faithfully stick to the message that he is given from God (46:9), follow Allah's duty for him (30:30), and work hard (66:9). In Surah 33, Allah tells Muhammad that he can take women as wives as long as he pays their dowry or if they are "prisoners of war." He can also marry his cousins, and any woman he wants "who dedicates her soul to the Prophet."

Muhammad's followers are told to visit the Prophet's home only when they have permission, to arrive right at meal time (not before), leave quickly after the meal, and avoid "familiar talk" with the Prophet. It is said that "such (behavior) annoys the Prophet: he is ashamed to dismiss you, but God is not ashamed (to tell you) the truth."

3. **Quran.** The Quran also takes up itself as a subject. Satan, we are told, is not the author. Muhammad could not be the author either, since, the Quran argues, he was completely illiterate. Only Allah could have produced such a book. The Quran says of itself that it is clear, understandable, written in pure Arabic, free from error, and that it contains the universal message, one that will guide its hearers into health and into eternal salvation.

4. **Biblical Material.** The Quran gives considerable attention to various Old and New Testament figures. Much of it is derived from Christian and Jewish apocryphal sources. Muslims claim that Islam started with creation and that Allah revealed himself to Jews and Christians, though both groups altered their Scriptures. Muslims use this to explain why Old and New Testament accounts of people and events often differ radically from how they are reported in the Quran.

Of biblical figures, Moses gets the most mention, with over 500 verses or almost ten percent of the text dealing with him. The Quran also gives information about Noah, Abraham, Joshua, David, Jesus, Mary, and others. Muslims find it easy to draw comparisons between Muhammad and Moses the lawgiver, and also with King David, the warrior for God.

5. **Jesus.** The Quran treats Jesus with great respect, as a prophet, teacher, and as a Sign from God. It also states that Jesus was born of the Virgin Mary, performed miracles, and that His followers were called Muslims. The Quran also states that it is a serious error to think that Jesus is the Son of God or that God is a trinity of three Persons, as in Christian tradition. For the Quran, Jesus is a prophet, but no more than that.

As said earlier, Muslims do not believe that Jesus died on the Cross. In Surah 4:157, one of the famous verses of the Quran, it speaks about enemies of Allah who insulted the Virgin Mary and who brag: "We killed Christ Jesus the son of Mary, the Apostle of God." The text then reads: "but they killed him not, nor crucified him, but so it was made to appear to them, and those who differ therein are full of doubts, with no (certain) knowledge, but only conjecture to follow, for of a surety they killed him not."

6. **True Believers.** Hundreds of verses in the Quran are devoted to a portrait of the true believer. The vast majority of passages deal with behavior, both with the path that is right, and the path that is wrong. This is in keeping with the common assertion that Islam is a religion about the right path, much more than it is a religion about right ideas.

Even though Islam is a religion of law, the Quran is focused more on the larger principles behind the law. These have to do, first of all, with positive things that are expected of all Muslims. The Muslim is a follower of Allah and fears him, and has turned from all false gods. The believer patterns his life after the model of the prophet Muhammad.

The Muslim is a person of prayer and contemplation. He or she is peaceful, faithful, humble, and forgiving. True believers strive to do good works and protect one another. Muslims are to be charitable, according to the Quran, and are to be united in their faith. The disciple of Allah engages in fasting and follows Allah's will on proper marriages and proper inheritance laws. Believers are to remember the rewards of heaven and the pains of hell.

Resistance to evil and sin also identifies the true believer. The Quran teaches that Muslims are to avoid gambling and drinking. Usury is a sin. Certain foods are forbidden, as in orthodox Judaism. Muslim males cannot have more than four wives. Allah's followers should avoid contact with skeptics and should avoid being too inquisitive about their faith. Sexual lust is wrong, and therefore female believers are to dress modestly.

The Quran warns about the dangers of excess in religion. Muhammad said one time that there were going to be no monks in Islam, referring to a celibate priesthood. This idea of excess also involves avoiding certain ideas. Thus, Surah 4:171 states: "O People of the Book! Commit no excesses in your religion: Nor say of God aught but the truth. Christ Jesus the son of Mary was (no more than) an apostle of God. Say not 'Trinity': desist: it will be better for you: for God is one God: Glory be to Him: (far exalted is He) above having a son."

7. **Unbelievers.** The whole human setting of the Quran involves the storm created by Muhammad's prophetic call to decision. His message creates two options: belief or

unbelief. There is considerable discussion of those that the Quran calls hypocrites and unbelievers.

Those who reject Allah's message are deaf, blind, and full of disease. They are arrogant, foolish, hate the truth, live in delusion, and their prayers are in vain. The unbeliever is a liar, coward, vain, and a deceiver. Muslims should avoid unbelievers, given their perversity. They will be sent into the depths of hell unless they repent.

8. **Heaven, Hell and Judgment Day.** The Quran gives enormous weight to life after death. There are hundreds of verses about paradise, the pains of hell, and the reality of a Final Judgment by God. Though Muslim scholars debate to what extent certain verses about heaven and hell are to be taken literally, the overall message is clear. Heaven is pictured as a garden paradise, with mansions, fountains, food and drink, sexual pleasure, where believers are full of happiness, peace, and joy in the presence of God.

The Quran draws hell as a place of blazing, eternal fire. The unbelievers will taste the boiling fluids of hell, with their faces covered in flame. They will wear garments of fire, will live in eternal regret at the folly of their rebellion against Allah, and will beg for destruction. The Day of Judgment is an absolute certainty, according to the Quran, though the righteous have no reason to fear. Justice will be done and human deeds will be weighed in the balance, when the Last Trumpet sounds.

CHAPTER FOUR

Muslims

The People Called Muslims

Understanding Islam involves coming to grips with the story of Islam through the centuries, the various divisions among Muslims that shape their internal understanding, and a sense of the presence of Islam both globally and in the United States. As well, our appreciation for Islam depends on grasping the major factors that shape the daily life of the Muslim, at home, at work, and in society.

Fifty Key Events in Muslim History

In any overview of a world religion, one has to have some sense of the big picture. To that end, we can give brief attention to fifty of the most significant events in Muslim history since the death of the prophet Muhammad in A.D 632. These dates give one a sense of the breadth of Islamic life and the shape of response in the non-Muslim world to the spread of Islam.

1. 634 Death of Abu Bakr, the first *caliph* or successor to Muhammad
2. 637 Capture of Jerusalem by Muslim leaders
3. 661 Assassination of Ali, the fourth caliph to Muhammad
4. 680 Murder of Husain, a son of Ali
5. 690 Construction of the Dome of the Rock in Jerusalem
6. 728 Death of Hasan al-Basri, early Sufi leader

7. 732 Muslims defeated at Battle of Tours
8. 750 Rise of the Abbasid Dynasty, based in Baghdad
9. 767 Death of Abu Hanifah, the great legal scholar
10. 925 Death of Abu Bakr al-Razi, one of the great doctors of medicine
11. 950 Death of Al-Farabi, the Muslim Aristotle
12. 1037 Death of Avicenna, a great Islamic philosopher
13. 1099 Crusaders capture Jerusalem
14. 1111 Death of al-Ghazali, second to the Prophet as spiritual leader
15. 1197 Saladin recaptures Jerusalem
16. 1258 Mongols sack Baghdad
17. 1300 Rise of Ottoman Empire
18. 1315 Death of Raymond Lull, Christian missionary to Islam
19. 1453 Ottoman Turks capture Constantinople—renamed Istanbul
20. 1492 End of Muslim Spain
21. 1517 Salim I conquers Egypt
22. 1520 Rise of Sulayman the Magnificent, the Ottoman emperor
23. 1563 Akbar gains power in India
24. 1707 Decline of Muslim power in India
25. 1798 Napoleon in Egypt
26. 1803 Wahhabi movement gains control in Saudi Arabia
27. 1830 France occupies Algeria
28. 1881 British take control of Egypt
29. 1902 Qasim Amin pioneers feminism in Egypt
30. 1910 Oil prospects in Persia
31. 1924 Secularization of Turkey

32. 1928 Muslim Brotherhood founded
33. 1932 Political independence in Iraq
34. 1947 Creation of Pakistan
35. 1948 Founding of the State of Israel
36. 1962 Algeria gains independence
37. 1964 Formation of the Palestinian Liberation Organization
38. 1967 Six Day War between Israel and Egypt
39. 1973 October War between Israel and Arabs
40. 1977 Anwar Sadat makes peace with Israel
41. 1979 Islamic revolution in Iran
42. 1979 USSR invades Afghanistan
43. 1982 Israeli invasion of Lebanon
44. 1982 Assassination of Anwar Sadat
45. 1987 Intifada begins in Palestine
46. 1991 Gulf War to liberate Kuwait
47. 1993 Bombing of the World Trade Center
48. 2000 Breakdown of Israel-Palestine peace talks
49. 2001 September 11—Attack on America
50. 2001 October 7—USA launches military campaign in Afghanistan

Several themes emerge from an examination of these 50 key events. First, it is obvious that **Islam has spread, at least in part, through military might.** In fact, the Muslim armies were so powerful that within a hundred years of the Prophet's death, the Islamic empire extended from the edge of China on the east, across the upper part of Africa, to Spain on the west. This is a military conquest almost unmatched in the history of the world.

Second, there is the **corresponding reality of the**

conquest of Muslims by others. The sword has cut both ways. Richard the Lion-Hearted, the famous Crusader, showed no mercy to Muslims, even when they surrendered, even after he promised them safety under his rule. Contemporary Islam has also known military defeat, thanks to empire-building at the hands of the British, French, Germans, and other powers.

Third, the key events also illustrate that **Islam has offered a rich intellectual heritage to the world.** This has come in terms of art, philosophy, architecture, medicine, jurisprudence, theology, mathematics, and science. In fact, when the Crusaders invaded Muslim lands, under orders to overthrow the barbarians, they were actually astonished at the high level of culture of Islam.

Fourth, **Muslim leaders have often been politically astute,** given the fact that they have had to run empires across vast distances, under diverse social climates, various linguistic realities, and changing military and economic conditions. The staying power of Islamic political life is shown best by the fact that the Muslim Ottoman Empire lasted over six centuries.

There is also a sense, however, that Muslim history illustrates a real decline in power and influence, even before the rise of the Ottoman sultans in the late thirteenth century. To some extent, Muslims continue to struggle with the loss of the "golden age" of Islam and debate among themselves about how to revive those days. A few brave Muslim intellectuals have risked death by calling for focus on internal reasons for Islamic decline rather than blaming Israel and the United States.

The Branches of Islam

Like all religions, Islam has not been able to retain its original unity. In fact, within a generation of the Prophet's death, Muslims were at war with each other over political leadership and the proper interpretation of Islamic spirituality. Muslims can be grouped under four major branches, with the three largest belonging to the more orthodox stream of Islam.

The three biggest branches are: (a) Sunni, (b) Shia, also known as Shiite, and (c) Sufi. Sunni Islam represents the largest grouping in Islam. Of the world's 1.2 billion Muslims, over one billion are **Sunni,** which is about nine in ten Muslims. Sunni Muslims trace themselves back to the Prophet but separate from Shia Muslims over the question of proper authority in Islam, the shape of Islamic law, and the nature of salvation.

There are 170 million **Shia or Shiite** Muslims globally. Though they represent a minority among the three main Islamic groups, the Shia version of Islam became the most well-known in the West after the Islamic revolution in Iran in 1979. The Shah of Iran was deposed and the Ayatollah Khomeni, the well-known Muslim leader, returned from exile in France to run the country.

In Sunni Islam, the *imam* is the person who leads prayer in the mosque. The same word in Shia Islam stands both for leaders like the Ayatollah but, most importantly, for the succession of singular figures said to be chosen by Allah to guide Islam in its earliest and most important years. One Shia group believes there were seven imams, while another extends the number to twelve. In each group the last imam is believed to be alive, but he has been placed in a state of hiddenness by Allah.

Shia Muslims give enormous significance to the martyrdom of Husein, whose father Ali, was the son-in-law of the Prophet. Husein and fellow Muslims were slaughtered by Sunni Muslims at Kerbala in Iraq on the tenth day of the Muslim month of Muharran in A.D. 680. Every year Shia Muslims engage in eleborate rituals to honor Husein's memory. Shia pilgrims travel to his shrine in Kerbala every year.

The **Sufis** represent the mystical side of Islam. Today, they number over 240 million throughout the world. Sufism emerged when Islam became decadent, materialistic, and lazy in the twilight years of the earliest Muslim dynasties. Al-Ghazzali, the great Islamic devotional writer, turned to Sufism as an alternative to the speculative, uncertain paths of philosophy and reason. The Sufi path is best known through the "whirling dervish," a type of dance used to resist outside stimuli and focus on the mind of Allah.

A fourth major branch of Islam involves a whole subset of groups that are viewed as heretical by most Muslims. The most famous of these so-called Muslim sects are: (a) the **Bahai,** (b) the **Ahmadis,** and (c) the **Druze.** All three groups are viewed with suspicion by most Muslims, but Bahais and the Ahmadis, in particular, have been subject to terrible persecution, even martyrdom. The Druze number about a million followers and are primarily located in Lebanon, Syria, and Palestine.

Bahais focus on their leader Baha'u'llah (1817–1892) as the final prophet for mankind, while the Druze believe the same of al-Hakim, an Egyptian of the eleventh century.

The Ahmadi movement was founded by Mirza Ghulam Ahmad Qadiyani (d. 1908), who also was proclaimed as the ultimate prophet, a notion contrary to the prevailing Muslim view that Muhammad is the "seal" of the prophets.

Muslims in the Global Context

One in every six persons on the planet is a Muslim. Islam is the second largest religion, with over one billion followers. There are Muslims in all the distinct nations of the world. Islam is truly a global religion, even though it is often dismissed as an Arab religion, a view countered by the fact that there are more non-Arab Muslims in Indonesia than there are Arab Muslims in any individual Arab nation.

From the beginning, **Muslims have viewed the world in two parts: those areas under the control of Islam and those outside.** In terms of the current global situation, the *CIA Factbook* lists 234 nations. Of these, Islam is the majority religion in 48 different countries, and a significant minority religion in another 26 nations. This means that Islam has a powerful presence in almost one third of the countries in the world.

The countries where Islam is in the majority are: Afghanistan, Albania, Algeria, Azerbaijan, Bahrain, Bangladesh, Brunei, Cocos (Keeling) Islands, Comoros, Djibouti, Egypt, Gambia, Gaza Strip, Guinea, Indonesia, Iran, Iraq, Jordan, Kazakhstan, Kuwait, Kyrgyzstan, Lebanon, Libya, Maldives, Mali, Mauritania, Mayotte, Morocco, Niger, Nigeria, Oman, Pakistan, Qatar, Saudi Arabia, Senegal, Sierra Leone, Somalia, Sudan, Syria, Tajikistan, Tunisia, Turkey,

Turkmenistan, United Arab Emirates, Uzbekistan, West Bank, Western Sahara, and Yemen.

Muslims represent a significant minority in the following nations: Benin, Bosnia and Herzegovina, Burkina Faso, Chad, Cote d'Ivoire, Cyprus, Eritrea, Ethiopia, Georgia, Ghana, Guinea-Bissau, India, Israel, Liberia, Macedonia, Malawi, Malaysia, Mauritius, Mozambique, Singapore, Suriname, Swaziland, Tanzania, Uganda, Yugoslavia, and Zambia.

The term minority can be misleading, since there are over 100 million Muslims in India. While the Middle East constitutes the heartland of Islam, the largest number of Muslims are found in Bangladesh, India, Indonesia, and Pakistan. In fact, over 40% of the entire Muslim population of the world is located in these four countries.

Islam in the United States

There are about six million Muslims in America, and there are estimates that within fifteen years Islam will bypass Judaism as the second largest religious grouping in America, next to Christianity. Muslims first came to America as slaves from Africa in the late 1700s. Muslim immigration began in the late nineteenth century, continuing in two surges just before and after World War I, after World War II, and again when President Johnson relaxed immigration laws in 1967.

Islam first came to public attention in America when Alexander Russell Webb, a Muslim convert, defended Islam at the first Parliament of the World's Religions held in Chicago in 1893. Webb helped build the first mosque in the USA. When Muslims immigrated to the American midwest in the early 1900s, mosques were built first in

Ross, North Dakota, and then one in Highland Park, Michigan, in 1919.

The various branches of Islam are all represented in America. Sunni Muslims dominate, as in the rest of the Muslim world. There are a number of Shia mosques and centers throughout America, including a branch of the Ismaeli group that follows Prince Aga Khan. There are also over forty separate Sufi groups active in the country, including the Sufi Order brought to America in 1910 by its founder, Pir Hazrat Inayat Khan.

The rise of the Black Muslim movement represents a fascinating aspect of Islam in the United States. Its roots lie in a resurgence of Black nationalism at the turn of the twentieth century, symbolized most significantly in the work of Marcus Garvey (1887–1940), a central figure in the Rastafarian movement, and Noble Drew Ali (1886–1929), founder of the Moorish Science Temple, another Black nationalist group.

Black nationalism took its formative shape through the influence of Fard Muhammad, who started preaching the Black Muslim message in Detroit in July 1930, and founded the Nation of Islam (NOI). Although he disappeared after four years, he influenced a man named Elijah Muhammad who heard Fard in 1930. Elijah Muhammad, born in 1897, accepted Fard's message about the supremacy of the Black race and the devilish nature of the white race.

Elijah Muhammad moved to Chicago in 1932 and led the NOI movement until his death in 1975. He was a controversial leader, not only because of his racist views, but also due to his extra-marital affairs that shocked his Nation of Islam, including Malcolm X, one of Elijah Muhammad's most famous followers. Malcolm X, born as Malcolm Little in 1925, converted to Islam in 1948, joined the NOI in 1953, and became a leader in the movement.

In April 1963, Malcolm X confronted Elijah about his adultery and the leader simply tried to rationalize his behavior. That led to some estrangement between the two, heightened by comments Malcolm X made about President Kennedy's assassination in November. Malcolm X left the Nation of Islam in early 1964, and was killed by three of its radical members on February 21, 1965.

The role of Malcolm X was then picked up by Louis Farrakhan (b. May 11, 1933) who became Elijah's National Minister in 1965 and minister of the movement's famous mosque in Harlem. After Elijah's death ten years later, Farrakhan had increasing disagreements with Wallace Deen Muhammad, Elijah's son and successor. From 1975 through 1985, Wallace steered the Nation of Islam on a more moderate course, shut it down in 1985, and emerged as a major Sunni leader in the United States.

These changes did not sit well with Farrakhan, who declared in November of 1977 that he was re-creating the Nation of Islam on the more radical teachings of Elijah Muhammad. In the last quarter of a century Farrakhan has become one of the most powerful and controversial Black leaders in America. On October 6, 1995, he led the Million Man March for Blacks in Washington. That same year, his infamy grew as he offered O. J. Simpson's attorneys the protection of the Nation of Islam. There was also news of a plot to kill him by the daughter of Malcolm X, who believed that Farrakhan was behind the assassination of her father.

The Shape of a Muslim Life

This chapter gives some sense of the breadth of Islamic history, the various divisions within Islam, and some of the significant aspects of the Muslim story in the United States. Apart from all of this complexity, what can be said about the common patterns in the Muslim's personal, social, economic, and moral life? Obviously, no two Muslims are alike. In spite of this, what can be generally expected as one becomes friends with a Muslim on the streets of Washington or Cairo or in Jammu in northern India?

Beyond the rhythms of Islamic religious life, we can expect the Muslim to be hospitable, especially in the Arab world. Our Muslim friend will obey the dietary laws of Islam, so we will not be served alcohol or pork. We will not be invited to gamble. If we are invited to the Muslim's home, we should avoid making comment on the person's possessions, since that would be an indication that you want these for your home.

If we talk ethics with our Muslim friend, there will be strong objection to abortion, suicide, and homosexuality, though Arab males are very demonstrative in their friendships. Muslims have some openness to birth control. We might notice some charms and amulets in the Muslim home, though these are generally frowned upon by the tradition. It would be very rude for us to show the bottom of our feet to any Muslim or greet him with the left hand.

If we are expecting promptness, we might be disappointed. There is a very relaxed attitude towards time in much of the Islamic world, especially in the Middle East and Africa. The phrase "if Allah wills" might accompany

any suggestions about time commitments. We can expect our Muslim friend to be tough in bartering, but Islam demands honesty once agreements are made. No interest is to be charged on any business transactions.

There is a good chance that our Muslim friend will not like being pushed into a corner intellectually. He does not want to lose face in a debate. He cannot understand why the West is so unsympathetic toward Islam and ignorant about its respect for human rights, honoring of the woman's proper role in society, and commitment to spread Islam to the whole world, as the Prophet commanded.

Most **Muslims regard themselves in unity with the whole Islamic community,** even as they express disagreements with those branches of Islam not their own. They harbor a sense of anger over Western mistreatment of Muslims, particularly in the case of the Palestinians. We may see overt anti-Semitism, particularly in myths about a global Jewish conspiracy.

Our Muslim friend will not tolerate any attacks on the credibility of the Prophet or the Quran. For him, as for most Muslims, these are fundamentals not up for debate. He cannot understand why we cannot see the beauty of the Prophet and the scientific miracle of the Quran. How could we possibly believe in a Trinity, he might ask, or that Jesus died on a cross, or that an idol is to be worshiped? He is sure that Islam will eventually triumph over all ideologies, including those of the United States. Despite some apparent jealousy over American power, he really believes that the message of the Quran is Allah's word to the whole world.

Countries and Freedom

The ratings on rights and freedom are those of Freedom House. On a scale of 1–7, the lower the number the better the rating for political and civil rights. NF=Not Free PF=Partly Free F=Free

Muslim Country	% Muslim	Political Rights	Civil Rights	Freedom Rating
Afghanistan	99%	7	7	NF
Albania	70%	4	5	PF
Algeria	99%	6	5	NF
Azerbaijan	93%	6	4	PF
Bahrain	70%	7	6	NF
Bangladesh	83%	3	4	PF
Brunei	67%	7	5	NF
Comoros	98%	6	4	PF
Djibouti	94%	4	6	PF
Egypt	94%	6	5	NF
The Gambia	90%	5	4	PF
Guinea	85%	6	5	NF
Indonesia	88%	4	4	PF
Iran	99%	6	6	NF
Iraq	97%	7	7	NF
Jordan	92%	4	4	PF
Kazakhstan	47%	6	5	NF
Kuwait	85%	4	5	PF
Kyrgyzstan	75%	5	5	PF
Lebanon	70%	6	5	NF
Libya	97%	7	7	NF
Maldives	99%	6	5	NF
Mauritania	100%	6	5	NF

Muslim Country	% Muslim	Political Rights	Civil Rights	Freedom Rating
Mali	90%	3	3	F
Mayotte	97%	1	2	F
Morocco	99%	5	4	PF
Niger	80%	5	5	PF
Nigeria	50%	4	3	PF
Oman	75%	6	6	NF
Pakistan	97%	7	5	NF
Qatar	95%	6	6	NF
Saudi Arabia	100%	7	7	NF
Senegal	92%	4	4	PF
Sierra Leone	60%	3	5	PF
Somalia	99%	7	7	NF
Sudan	70%	7	7	NF
Syria	90%	7	7	NF
Tajikistan	85%	6	6	NF
Tunisia	98%	6	5	NF
Turkey	99%	4	5	PF
Turkmenistan	89%	7	7	NF
United Arab Emirates	96%	6	5	NF
Uzbekistan	88%	7	6	NF
Western Sahara	100%	7	6	NF
Yemen	99%	5	6	NF

CHAPTER FIVE

Women

Women in Islam

The immense volume of literature on the subject of women in Islam reveals a dramatic division of opinion. The difference is so extreme that one wonders if the same subject is being debated.

On the one hand, orthodox Muslims believe that women gain true freedom in Islam, that the Prophet liberated females, that there is essential equality between males and females, and that non-Muslims have misunderstood the whole topic. On the opposite extreme, critics of Islam argue that women are in bondage in Islam, that the Prophet was a chauvinist, and that the Quran contains very offensive material about woman. Many non-Muslims believe that Islamic law and tradition treat women as second-class citizens, and that women are subject to abuse in most Muslim countries of the world.

Orthodox Islamic Ideals

In understanding the place of women in Islam, we can start with a listing of very positive ideals that are taught in orthodox Islam. These principles may not always be followed, but they present the orthodox Islamic teaching in its best light. Here are fifteen key points gathered from various Muslim authors, including Hammudah Abdalati and Jamal A. Badawi, two respected Muslim authorities.

1. The Quran teaches against the view that women are inferior to men.
2. Islam stopped the practice of female infanticide in the Arab world.
3. Women are equal to men but have different roles.
4. Women are allowed to receive education just like men.
5. Women are to be given freedom of expression.
6. Marriage and family life are very sacred.
7. Motherhood is given incredible honor in Islam.
8. Husbands are to love their wives and treat them kindly.
9. Husbands are to make sure their wives are satisfied sexually.
10. The separation of females in worship is done for reasons of purity.
11. Divorce is to be allowed only when absolutely necessary.
12. Women receive a just inheritance in Islamic family law.
13. Veiling of Muslim women is done for protection and purity.
14. The seclusion of women is practiced for reasons of social purity.
15. Polygamy is allowed only if all wives can be supported and loved.

In one of Badawi's essays on the status of women he quotes Surah 4:1 from the Quran: "O mankind! reverence your Guardian-Lord, who created you from a single person, created, of like nature, His mate, and from them twain scattered (like seeds) countless men and women."

Of this passage, Badawi writes: "In the midst of the darkness that engulfed the world, the divine revelation echoed in the wide desert of Arabia with a fresh, noble, and universal message to humanity." He then cites an unnamed scholar on the same text: "It is believed that there is no text, old or new, that deals with the humanity of the woman from all aspects with such amazing brevity, eloquence, depth, and originality as this divine decree."

Despite this glowing rhetoric, the debate about women in Islam is not settled so quickly or simply. Difficult questions remain about the above points, and other concerns are raised as well, including criticisms of the way the Prophet treated women. Are women really viewed as equal in the Quran? Is veiling and seclusion truly helpful to women? Is polygamy compatible with the freedom of women?

The Quran on Women

Some of the lofty principles noted above find solid support in the Quran. **The Quran affirms the unity of males and females in the original creation by Allah.** There are at least fifteen passages in the Quran that make this point, including Surah 7:189, which reads: "It is He Who created you from a single person, and made his mate of like nature, in order that he might dwell with her (in love)."

Further, the Quran teaches that **women will be rewarded for their labor by Allah,** just like men. "For Muslim men and women—for believing men and women, for devout men and women, for true men and women, for men and women who are patient and constant, for men and women who humble themselves, for men and women who give in Charity, for men and women who fast (and deny themselves), for men and women who guard their chastity, and for men and women who engage much in God's praise—for them has God prepared forgiveness and great reward." (33:35)

The Quran also describes husbands and wives as friends (4:36), and says that there is to be "tranquility, love and mercy" between them (30:21). In heaven, there will be delight, love, and joy between spouses (36:55–57, 55:51–53). If divorce occurs in this life, women are to be treated with grace (2:237) and justice (2:231 and 65:2), and there should be arbitration in conflict (4:35).

Critics of Islam point to other passages, however, to complain about the status and treatment of women in the Quran. The dominant charges are: (1) the Quran teaches that the testimony of women is worth only half that of males; (2) the Quran grants more power to husbands in the divorce process than is given to wives; (3) the Quran often grants greater inheritance rights to males than females; (4) the Quran grants men access to female slaves for sexual purposes; (5) the Quran allows polygamy for males; and (6) the Quran actually teaches that husbands are superior to wives and can beat them.

Muslim apologists admit to the factual reality of these points but seek to blunt criticism by arguing that (a) the Quranic teaching improved the status of women in contrast to pre-Islamic Arabic life, (b) social conditions explain the need for polygamy, or for the differences about legal testimony and inheritance rights, (c) military realities of Muhammad's day warrant the use of female slaves, and (d) Allah's Word is to be trusted and not treated with suspicion and doubt.

The idea that a husband can beat his wife is rooted in Surah 4:34, which reads: "Men are the protectors and maintainers of women, because God has given the one more (strength) than the other, and because they support them from their means." The verse continues: "As to those women on whose part ye fear disloyalty and ill-conduct, admonish them (first), (Next), refuse to share their beds, (And last) beat them (lightly)."

Many ancient and modern Muslim authorities have accepted the plain meaning of the text. For example, Abdullatif Mushtahiri, a contemporary scholar, writes: "If admonishing and sexual desertion fail to bring forth results and the woman is of a cold and stubborn type, the Quran bestows on man the right to straighten her out by way of punishment and beating, provided he does not break her bones nor shed blood. Many a wife belongs to this querulous type and requires this sort of punishment to bring her to her senses!"

Muhammad and Women

The teaching of the Prophet on women and the example he set with women is crucial in understanding the Islamic heritage about women. Obviously, Muhammad would affirm all of the ideal principles noted earlier. Muslims love to cite stories from the *hadith* about his care for girls, his concern about women who were being mistreated, and about his tender relations with Khadijah, his first wife.

Critics of Islam target Muhammad for some of the same things noted in the Quranic material. Thus, Muhammad is viewed as a male chauvinist because of his views on inheritance rights, legal value of a woman's testimony, male dominance in divorce proceedings, and the inferiority of women. Critics also question Muhammad's moral character in terms of his engagement in polygamy, sexual use of female slaves, and defense of the Quran when it teaches that wives can be beaten.

Muslim apologists use the same arguments to defend the Prophet as they do for defending the Quran. However, they also have to address other things that surfaced in the course of Muhammad's life. These include complaints that the Prophet: (a) taught that there are more women in hell than men, (b) believed brief contractual marriages are sometimes right, given the sexual needs of males, (c) married one of his wives when she was just six years old, (d) married his own stepson's wife, (e) taught that women are mentally inferior to men, and (f) believed that the prayer of a man is invalid if a donkey, dog, or woman walks in front of him while praying.

Contrary to what non-Muslims might think, these allegations were not invented by enemies of Muhammad. Islamic scholars grant that each point arises out of genuine *hadith* about the Prophet. In other words, there is no dispute over the basic facts. The differences come over how to interpret them, whether a person accepts or rejects the Prophet's teaching, and whether his behavior is justified or condemned.

For the orthodox Muslim, it is absolutely unthinkable that the Prophet can be wrong in his views or in his deeds. So, if the Prophet taught, for example, that women outnumber men in hell, then that is a truth that is to be accepted. If he taught that women are mentally inferior, that is the case. If he advocated brief contractual marriages, then he was right to do so. Who is anyone to question the word of the Prophet?

The story of Muhammad's marriage to Aisha when she was six illustrates how one's fundamental worldview determines perspective and judgment. According to the *hadith,* Muhammad did in fact marry her when she was six, though he did not consummate his marriage until she was nine.

Muslim scholars have gone to great lengths to defend the Prophet. Some argue that Aisha was much older, in her mid-teens, when the Prophet first slept with her. Another author states that by marrying Aisha so early, she was given a longer time to know the great Prophet.

Other Muslims simply declare that Allah gave Aisha to the Prophet at age six in marriage, and that there is absolutely nothing wrong with him sleeping with her at age nine. This was the will of Allah, the perfect Creator, for his sinless Prophet. One writer states: "Only in Islam can one with good conscience accept 'the whole package' without ignorantly or hypocritically denying things that they don't like. This is how true internal peace and balance are achieved."

The Issue of Female Circumcision

In recent years the world community has been alarmed by the practice of female circumcision, which is also known as Female Genital Mutilation (FGM). This ritual is done in more than thirty countries worldwide. It involves several medical procedures, which include removal of some or all of the female genitalia. Scholars suggest that two million girls go through this rite every year, and about 15% die as a result.

Muslim leaders throughout history have defended female circumcision on the basis of various alleged sayings of Muhammad. Even in recent years these sayings of Muhammad, and some material in the Quran, have been used to defend both male and female circumcision. About a decade ago, some Egyptian clerics wanted to have a *fatwa* (ruling) that called for the death penalty for a Muslim judge who did not favor male circumcision. An Egyptian court ruled that female circumcision could not be outlawed because of certain sayings of the Prophet that seemed to favor it.

Some Muslim leaders seek to defend female circumcision by arguing that it protects young girls from sexual temptation. One writer argued that the experience of going through the rite is actually beneficial in other ways, too, since the young girl receives presents, and she is surrounded by a loving community, and the incredible

Militant Islam: The Taliban on Women

- Cannot receive education
- Cannot be employed
- Must remain at home unless absolutely necessary
- No female doctors
- Cannot associate with any male who is not a relative
- Cannot wear nail polish or any makeup
- Cannot have hair cut
- Must wear the veil (*burqa*) at all times outside the home
- Violation of dress code will result in public lashings
- Breaking of sexual rules will result in stoning
- Transported by special buses with windows covered

support gives her better sense of self. Other Muslim leaders challenge the view that Islam mandates female circumcision.

Women in Modern Islam

As complex as the debate is over the ideals of Islamic orthodoxy, it is obviously much more difficult to write with accuracy about the actual realities of life for Muslim women in a global perspective. Given the number of Muslim women in the world, the diversity of Muslim states, the power of feminism, the only thing that can be written with certainty is that no one picture can capture what it is like to be a Muslim woman in our day. Here are some snapshots that capture the diverse realities gathered from books, newspaper reports, and websites.

- In Britain and other western countries, secular women are turning to Islam as an alternative to a materialistic culture that treats women as objects for sexual gratification.
- In Jordan, rape victims find themselves cut off from their families and even killed because of the shame brought to the home because of the loss of virginity.
- Sister Power! operates a web site to bring skilled Muslim women together to increase job opportunities and increase business success.
- In Saudi Arabia, rich princesses obey Muslim law while at home and then adopt a western mindset as soon as their private jets whisk them away for weekend parties in Paris and London.

- In one Middle East country, a woman had acid thrown on her face because she allowed a wisp of hair to appear from beneath her head covering.
- Fareena Alam, a Bengali woman living in London, starts the web site "Islam—The Modern Religion" at age 18. She believes that "Islam's attitude toward woman is a dream come true for anyone who is interested in equal rights and feminism."
- A Canadian woman converts to Islam from a liberal Protestant church. She loses her two children in a custody suit with her non-Muslim husband. At her mother's funeral, she is told by her uncle, a Christian pastor: "When we bury her, we bury you."
- Karamah, an organization of Muslim female lawyers, monitors human rights abuses from its base in Fairfax, Virginia. They protest abuses of women by Muslim leaders around the world.
- A Muslim woman from the Middle East decides to become a Christian. She is tortured for her decision and her face shows marks of the brutality. She flees to Canada to escape threats of death.
- In January 2000 the Taliban relaxed some of their rules about girls being educated, ignoring the establishment of private schools that allow girls to get an education.

CHAPTER SIX

Jihad and Terrorism

Jihad and September 11

September 11, 2001, has forever altered the significance of the word *jihad* to the modern world. While many Muslims assert that the word simply means spiritual struggle, militant Islam has a far more sinister understanding: "Holy War."

In February 1998, three and a half years before September 11, Osama bin Laden made his own views clear. Along with other extremists from Egypt, Pakistan, and Bangladesh, he issued a *fatwa* or ruling that called on Muslims "to kill the Americans and their allies—civilian and military." He said that this is "an individual duty for every Muslim who can do it in any country in which it is possible to do it." In the winter of 2001, Osama bin Laden told ABC News producer Rahimullah Yousafsai that he would kill his own children, if necessary, in order to hit American targets.

In contrast, the vast majority of Muslim states have opposed Osama bin Laden since September 11. Here is one news report of enormous significance for world peace: "Iran has vehemently condemned the suicidal terrorist attacks in the United States and has expressed its deep sorrow and sympathy with the American nation" (*Iran Today,* September 24, front page report). The governments of Bahrain, Egypt, Lebanon, Oman, Pakistan, Palestine, Qatar, Saudi Arabia, Turkey, United Arab Emirates, and Yemen also expressed their condemnation of the terrorist attacks.

American Muslim groups condemned the terrorist attack immediately. One prominent group issued this press release on September 12: "The Islamic Supreme Council of America (ISCA) categorically condemns yesterday's airline hijackings and attacks against the World Trade Center, the Pentagon, and all other targets. From coast to coast, we join our neighbors, co-workers and friends across ethnic, cultural and religious lines in mourning the devastating loss of precious life, which Islam holds as sacred. We pray for the thousands of innocent victims, for their families, for law enforcement and emergency workers, for stranded travelers, and for all whose confidence and security have been shaken. We pray that God's Infinite Mercy reaches us all."

The tragedies of September 11 have brought to the surface a long and bitter struggle between Muslims over the meaning of *jihad* and the nature of true Islam. These contemporary conflicts about Islam's real identity lie in ancient debates about the teaching of the Quran, the example of the Prophet, the legitimacy of non-Muslim governments, and the place of war in Islamic ideology.

Background to the Two Islams

The current debates between Muslims about *jihad* are better understood when the following crucial facts are noted. Anyone who reads even briefly on the history and nature of Islam will discover these items to be beyond dispute, though what these facts mean is a source of considerable debate.

- The Quran uses the term *jihad* in terms of personal spiritual struggle.
- The Quran also uses *jihad* about "holy war" or just war.
- The Prophet engaged in battles of war.
- The Prophet taught that Islam must be spread to the whole world.
- Islamic law justifies self-defense and certain acts of war.
- Muslims conquered non-Arab lands and peoples through war.
- Muslims divide the world into two: Islam and non-Islam.
- Many Muslims believe that all countries should follow Islamic law.
- Many Muslim countries are authoritarian rather than democratic and do not tolerate dissent.

Out of the mix of these realities has emerged two basically different perspectives among modern Muslims. The vast majority of Muslims believe that none of the above points justify terrorism. They believe that the Quranic defense of war does not apply to the attacks of September 11. They believe that Osama bin Laden would be condemned by the Prophet, that he has broken Islamic law, that he has disgraced Islam, and is doomed to eternal punishment.

Muslim extremists believe the opposite. They view their actions as a true *jihad* or "holy war" against infidels and the enemies of Islam. They believe it is right to target America, "the great Satan." Osama bin Laden believes that the Quran supports his campaign, that the Prophet would bless his cause, that Islamic law justifies his actions, and that Allah is on his side. We are left then with a world of two Islams.

Major Islamic Terrorist Groups

About 70 major terrorist groups operate in the world. Of these, more than 30 are Islamic in orientation. Of the rest, only a few are widely recognized, like the Irish Republican Army or the Aum group that spread poison gas in the Tokyo subway system. Among the Islamic groups, the most well known are:

- Abu Nidal Organization (aka Black September)
- Islamic Group or IG (aka Al-Gama'a al-Islamiyya)
- Armed Islamic Group
- Hamas
- Hizballah (Party of God, aka Islamic Jihad)
- al-Jihad (aka Islamic Jihad)
- al-Qaida (of Osama bin Laden)

Before September 11, Americans for the most part were not worried about such groups. Europeans had a far greater sensitivity to terrorism because of militant groups operating in Ireland and Spain. Israel had firsthand experience with all Islamic groups. America seemed safe, even after the attacks on American embassies in Kenya and Tanzania, and on the USS Cole in South Yemen.

Some lecturers on terrorism have stated that there was more chance of dying from a fall in your bathtub than from a terrorist attack. As absurd as it sounds now, that point had merit prior to September's attack. The U.S. State Department lists a total of 77 American casualties in terrorist attacks around the world from 1995 through 2000, and then, on one day, more than 5,000 died in the World Trade Center alone.

The Islamic terrorist groups have several aims: (a) use violence to bring their version of Islam to particular Muslim countries; (b) establish a Palestinian state; (c) destroy the State of Israel; (d) crush dissent against their views; and (e) attack the United States of America. These goals are expressed in the language of religious hatred. On Sunday, October 9, al-Jazeera satellite TV released a statement from Osama bin Laden that captures his style and ideology. Here are excerpts:

"America is filled with fear. America has been filled with horror from north to south and east to west, and thanks be to God what America is tasting now is only a copy of what we have tasted. God has blessed a group of vanguard Muslims to destroy America and may God bless them and allot them a supreme place in heaven.

"I swear to God that America will never dream of security or see it before we live it and see it in Palestine, and not before the infidels' armies leave the land of Muhammad, peace be upon him."

Of course, behind these words lie deeds of terror. Judith Miller reported from the Middle East for *The New York Times* for years and wrote about it in her book *God Has Ninety-Nine Names*. Her powerful prose captures the depth of tragedy and evil in militant Islam, whether in the Sudanese slave trade, the execution of moderates in Egypt, the slaughter of Kurdish Muslims in Iraq, the gang-rape of devout Muslim women in Algeria by Muslim extremists, or the killings of journalists in the same country (eighteen in 1994 alone), some by decapitation.

In the year prior to September 11, Israel was the target

of terrorism repeatedly. Suicide bombers attacked restaurants and busy shopping areas, killing and injuring dozens of citizens. In some instances, individual Jewish youths were shot or stoned to death near their homes. Terrorist groups claimed responsibility for some actions, but others appeared to be the work of lone assailants.

Understanding Islamic Terrorism

"How could they do it?" A year or so of planning, waiting in Florida, New Jersey or Maine—wherever—enjoying life in America, and then, the unimaginable: two planes into the World Trade Center, one into the Pentagon, and another brought down in a field in Pennsylvania. Our first response was a failure of imagination. This simply could not be happening. How could we understand it?

There are six different views of the events of September 11.

1. **Mental illness.** In this view, the terrorists are crazy, mad, insane. Nothing can explain what they did because their actions are outside any ordinary discourse of reason and sense. These deeds are irrational, beyond the understanding of any decent human being. These are monsters of insanity.

2. **Evil.** The terrorists are the embodiment of wickedness. Their behavior can only be explained on the grounds of hellish hate. These are people without conscience, who have no moral compass. They are fanatics whose hearts are darkened by their alliance with evil.

This interpretation must take serious note of the fact that the evil is done under the guise of good, in the name of Allah. This brings to mind the thesis of Phillip Hallie's book *The Paradox of Cruelty:* most evil is done with "good" intentions.

3. **Terrorist ideology.** To Osama bin Laden and his colleagues, there is no mystery to understanding why September 11 happened. The United States deserved what it got. It is an enemy of Allah, opposed to Islam, and worthy of destruction. Islamic terrorists believe what they are doing is right. Hundreds of thousands of young Muslim boys are being taught daily in this ideology. It will be their only schooling, and they are not allowed to ask questions.

4. **Islam-bashing.** This view contends the killings on September 11 prove once and for all that Islam is the religion of the sword. On this view, all Muslims are terrorists and Islam is the chief cause of the wickedness. Based on this, some Americans have attacked Muslims at will. One member of the Sikh faith, a religion very distinct from Islam, was killed on a street in Texas simply because his turban looked like that of the Taliban leaders.

5. **America-blaming.** From this interpretation, while the events of September 11 are wrong, America has created its own fate through its abuse of power, its arrogance as the only reigning superpower, and its military attacks on Muslim people. Further, American complicity in the abuse of Palestinians by Israel has created legitimate anger towards the USA.

6. **Failure in the Arab Muslim world.** The attack on America is, according to this view, a result of a Muslim ignorance that lacks the will or freedom to be self-critical. The hatred of America is fueled by their jealousy of the wealth and freedom of America in contrast to the poverty and dictatorship in the Muslim Arab world. Thus, America is blamed for calamity, oppression, and evil that is actually

caused by either the evil of Islamic dictatorships or the evil of Islamic militants.

This point has been articulated best by Kanan Makiya, author of the famous works *Republic of Fear* (on Saddam's Iraq) and *Cruelty and Silence,* a powerful protest against the silence of Arab intellectuals about the dark side of the militant Islamic Middle East. In a London *Observer* article on "Fighting Islam's Ku Klux Klan" Makiya writes of the incredible price that Muslims will pay if they "continue to wallow in the sense of one's own victimhood to the point of losing the essentially universal idea of human dignity and worth that is the only true measure of civility."

He continues: "Arabs and Muslims need today to face up to the fact that their resentment at America has long since become unmoored from any rational underpinnings it might once have had; like the anti-Semitism of the interwar years, it is today steeped in deeply embedded conspiratorial patterns of thought rooted in profound ignorance of how a society and a polity like the United States, much less Israel, functions." His article ends with these words:

"Muslims and Arabs have to be on the front lines of a new kind of war, one that is worth waging for their own salvation and in their own souls. And that, as good out-of-fashion Muslim scholars will tell you, is the true meaning of *jihad,* a meaning that has been hijacked by terrorists and suicide bombers and all those who applaud or find excuses for them. To exorcise what they have done in our name is the civilisational challenge of the twenty-first century for every Arab and Muslim in the world today."

Islam: A Religion of Peace?

President George W. Bush has stated publicly on several occasions that "Islam is a religion of peace." By this he was making reference to the Islam that condemns terrorism, to the millions of Muslims who deplore Osama bin Laden, and to the significant Islamic traditions that support peace between religions and between all peoples. The President was speaking of the Islam which has brought meaning and stability to the lives of millions of its followers.

September 11 proved that there is another Islam, that of the Muslims who readily kill in the name of Allah. The terrorists who hijacked one of the planes at Logan Airport in Boston left behind their instructions on what to do if a passenger interfered in their plot: "If God grants any one of you a slaughter, you should perform it as an offering on behalf of your father and mother, for they are owed by you. Do not disagree among yourselves, but listen and obey. If you slaughter, you should plunder those you slaughter, for that is a sanctioned custom of the Prophet's." When the President spoke of a peaceful Islam, Muslims of another stripe burned the American flag and dreamed of more attacks on America.

There is an Islam of peace. It is in the millions of Muslims who live every day in love and gentleness. It is in the Muslim praying five times a day for no more September 11s. It is in those mosques where clerics preach that Islam is not a religion of the sword. It is in those Afghans who know that Osama bin Laden has betrayed their country. It is in those Muslims who know that there is a hateful perversion of "Islam" that could not possibly be from Allah, the all-Merciful Creator.

CHAPTER SEVEN

Palestine

Israel and Palestine

Understanding Islam in modern times demands knowledge of the Palestinian issue and the way conflict over Palestine has shaped the self-identity of Muslims throughout the world. Public dialogue since September 11 has often raised the Palestinian question as a factor in understanding, and even defending, Islamic extremism and the nature of terrorism.

Thirty Key Dates in the Palestinian Conflict

Since the rise of Zionism in the late 1800s, there have been increasing conflicts between Jews and Arabs in Palestine. Here are 30 key dates:

1882 First wave of Jewish immigation to Palestine
1896 Theodore Herzl publishes *The Jewish State*
1897 First International Zionist Congress
1904 Second wave of Jewish immigration
1914 World War I begins
1917 Balfour declaration in support of Jewish state
1919 Third wave of Jewish immigration
1920 Palestine under control of British
1920 Formation of Haganah (Jewish underground army)
1924 Fourth wave of Jewish immigration
1929 Massacre of Jews in Hebron
1933 Hitler gains power in Germany
1933 Fifth wave of Jewish immigration
1939 World War II and Holocaust begins

1944 Jewish underground attacks British presence
1947 Palestinians reject UN plan of partition
1948 Proclamation of Jewish state
1948 War of Independence
1948 Massacre of Palestinians at Dir Yassin
1956 Sinai War
1964 Founding of the Palestine Liberation Organization
1967 Six Day War in June
1973 Yom Kippur War
1978 Camp David Accord (Arafat and Begin)
1982 Israel invades Lebanon
1987 Intifadah begins
1991 Iraq attacks Israel during Gulf War
1993 Palestinians and Jews agree to Oslo accords
2000 Arafat and Barak talks fail at Camp David
2000 Second Intifadah begins

Different Interpretations of the Palestinian Question

Study of the details of the history of the Palestinian question will leave anyone deeply depressed for several reasons. First, the conflict between Jew and Arab has been one full of blood. There have been five major wars between Jews and Arabs in the half century since the founding of the state of Israel in 1948.

Second, the history of the Palestinian conflict is one of missed opportunities. Things could have been different. Jews started to return to Palestine in the late 1800s. Throughout this 120-year period, certain roads were chosen by both Jew and Arab that ensured further conflict. The wrong voices were heard. The will for peace died. The sword of revenge was taken up repeatedly.

Third, any student of Israeli or Palestinian history will see immediately that ideological divisions run so deep that it is almost impossible to imagine a decisive turn towards peace. This involves: (a) radical differences in **religious** views, (b) competing **political** understandings, (c) divergent **historical** verdicts, and (d) opposing **moral** views about every aspect of the conflict.

The differences about Israel and Palestine can be expressed in four competing interpretations. Understanding the nature and power of these four views is a necessary first step for any understanding of the complex and tragic story of the Jewish and Arab conflict of the Middle East, a conflict that affects Jews and Muslims everywhere. For the sake of clarity, each of these positions is written in a voice of the advocate.

1. The dominant Jewish position (written in the voice of the advocate)

"The founding of the state of Israel is a moral and historical fact. Given the hatred Jews have encountered throughout history, and in the face of the Holocaust, the Jewish people had every right to re-create their homeland. This great victory for the world Jewish community occurred on May 15, 1948. For the first time in two thousand years, we were home.

"Tragically, the Arab world chose not to accept the proposal of the United Nations to have two separate states in Palestine. Instead, Arabs chose to fight Israel in 1948, and have done so ever since. The Arab world wants Israel to be destroyed. Four of the wars since independence in 1948 involved attack on Israel by Arabs, including Palestinians. Our invasion of Lebanon was a necessary measure to wipe out terrorist bases in that country.

"Israel's aggression against the Palestinians is about legitimate self-defense. We cannot be at peace with a people who hate us, who want us destroyed. The world must not give nation status to a terrorist people. The Palestinian mind has been corrupted by decades of racist hate towards the Jew and towards Israel, a hatred fueled by Islamic militants throughout the world.

"The events of September 11 have sadly brought to America what Israel has faced for years: the wanton killing of innocent people by terrorists driven by hate. We are grateful for the help of the United States in defending the freedom of Israel. You have been our strongest ally in our fight for survival. Together, we will stand strong against the forces that seek to destroy us.

"We hope, of course, that Palestinians will stop their hatred of Israel, affirm our right to nationhood, and cease their terrorist activities against Jews in Israel and throughout the world. We are ready to negotiate with Mr. Arafat at any time, providing that he and other Palestinians lay

Balfour Declaration of England 1917

His Majesty's Government views with favor the establishment in Palestine of a national home for the Jewish people, and will use their best endeavors to facilitate the achievement of this object, it being clearly understood that nothing shall be done which may prejudice the civil and religious rights of existing non-Jewish communities in Palestine or the rights and political status enjoyed by Jews in any other country.

down their rocks and their bombs. Their continued war on Israel shows their obsession with the destruction of our nation. We will not be moved."

2. The moderate Jewish position (written in the voice of the advocate)

"The birth of Israel is a joy to all Jews. It is a miracle from God who brought us back to our land. But with this incredible gift comes enormous moral and spiritual responsibility. We cannot allow the forces of anti-Semitism to blind us to commitment to the ideals that have been our beacon of light through the centuries as a people with no land.

"There is much in the birth of Israel that stains our purity. From the start, and through the last century, we gave no serious moral thought to the rights and needs of the Arabs who were already here when we started to come home. Menachim Begin, who later became prime minister, even engaged in terrorist acts against the British in the mid-1940s. We secretly conspired against Arabs even as we publicly said we wanted Palestinians to have their own state.

"While there is no excuse for the Arab attacks on our nation, there is also no justification for what we have done to the Palestinians. Our invasion of Lebanon in 1982 was an unjust attack on another nation. The Palestinians have a right to their own country. We must overcome our own bigotry and hatred.

"We are becoming a terrorist nation against the Palestinians. Our secret defense forces have blown up Palestinian militia headquarters. We have destroyed Palestinian homes. We have razed entire villages. Our soldiers have engaged in torture of Palestinians. We have our hired assassins. We have our own zealots who match Islamic terrorists word for word, deed for deed. All of this must stop."

3. The extreme Palestinian position (written in the voice of the advocate)

"Palestine has been a home of Arabs for hundreds of years. We lost our native land through Zionist aggression. We refused the United Nations' partition of our land because it was our land. The British dominated us by force and they left us to the Zionist Jews to do the same. Our country was stolen from us by the Jewish pig.

"We were attacked by the Jews throughout the 20th century. We engaged in *jihad* against them on four occasions because it is our duty to cleanse the earth of their filth. We will not stop until the Jews are forced into the ocean. The American fascists support Israel because America is run by Jews. The Jew runs the economies of the world, including Britain, Germany, and Japan.

"The Jews use the lie of the Holocaust to create sympathy for their cause. Hitler opposed the Jew for the same reason we do: the Jewish vermin will poison and destroy everything in their path. The Jews have even published their plans to run the world. Their leaders met and reported of their attempted conquest in their *Protocols of the Elders of Zion*.

"The attack on the World Trade Center is probably a Zionist plot, cooked up by the American CIA in bed with the Israeli Mossad. If it is the work of Osama bin Laden, well, American Jewry is getting what it deserves. Either way, it is really the fault of the Jew. Jews were told to stay home from the World Trade Center on that day. They will never stop oppressing us because they have always stood against Allah and his true followers.

"The Jewish leaders of Israel assault our holy places. They humiliate us at their checkpoints. They raid our lands and burn down our villages. They kill our leaders, rape our women, maim our children, torture our soldiers. They cut off our water supplies, keep us from work, shut down our schools, and grind us into poverty. Allah will inflict upon them the fires of eternal hell."

4. The moderate Palestinian position (written in the voice of the advocate)

"It is a historical fact that we were here long before the Jews arrived in 1882. We have a moral right to nationhood. However, our path to freedom demands that we recognize the nation of Israel. Whether we like it or not, Israel is here to stay. We must stop our hatred of Jews and our talk of wiping Israel off the map. We made a terrible error when we refused the U.N. offer of statehood in 1947.

"We have engaged in brutal acts against innocent Israelis. Every terrorist act has dulled whatever inclination Israel may have to grant us our own country. We have been our own worst enemies. We will not gain the international support we need until we stop our quest for blood. Osama bin Laden has hurt our cause and has brought great shame to Islam. We must not follow in his path.

"We have been racists against Israel. We have trusted anti-Semitic lies about Jews, including the bizarre theory that the Holocaust never happened. We stereotype Jews much like the rest of the world draws stereotypes of us. We will never learn to get along until we stop our bigotry and our hate. The throwing of stones must stop. Our bombing must stop.

"Following the way of Allah means we must be people of peace. Muhammad (Peace Be Upon Him) taught us that war is to be used only as a last resort. Many Jews of good will (People of the Book) know that we deserve our own land. It is time for Mr. Arafat to deal in good faith with Jewish leaders. The tragic events of September 11 show us that terror just breeds more terror. For the sake of our children, all children, let us return to the table of peace."

Responding to the Views

Anyone with any emotion and common sense will know that these views represent different universes. However, we cannot let that fact leave us in despair that no progress can be made. So, let me suggest some essentials in a proper response.

1. These four views are not an exhaustive look at the Palestinian question. For example, the reader might note the absence of a racist Jewish view that is parallel to the extreme Palestinian position. The reason for this is that racist perspectives are simply not popular among Jews in Israel or elsewhere. One exception is the material and views propounded by a Jewish terrorist group founded by Rabbi Meir Kahane, the victim of an assassin's bullet in November 1990.

2. It will be hard for many readers to imagine that some Muslims really employ such racist language about Jews. Tragically, Muslims have duplicated "Christian" anti-Semitism in their attack on Jews. The extreme Palestinian view is real and it is popular, just as Hitler's was real

and popular seventy-five years ago. Some Muslims have the same view of the Jews as Hitler did.

In fact, Jeffrey Goldberg wrote an article on Islamic extremism for the *New Yorker* magazine where he quotes a Muslim cleric from Egypt who had this to say: "Thanks to Hitler, of blessed memory, who on behalf of the Palestinians took revenge in advance, against the most vile criminals on the face of the earth. Although we do have a complaint against him, for his revenge was not enough." This is beyond vile.

3. No amount of racism will undo the proof that the Holocaust is a real event in history. The evidence about Hitler's extermination of the Jews is overwhelming except to the morally blind. The case for a Palestinian state is hurt by the prevalence of Holocaust denial or by conspiracy theories against Israel.

4. There is a great chasm, virtually unbridgeable, between extreme Jewish and Muslim views on Palestine. The divide between a moderate Palestinian approach and even the dominant Jewish position is less significant. It is out of the middle ground of the moderate positions that peace has the best opportunity. But, for both Arab and Jew, it will not be peace at any price.

5. What stands in the way of peace is that the violence on both sides is rooted in a hardness of heart that refuses to acknowledge that the "other" (whether Jew or Arab) is to be treated differently than this view of violence allows. Neither extreme wants to give ground by admitting fault, showing weakness, granting that the situation is complex, or that guilt is shared to any extent.

6. Many readers will be shocked by the moderate Jewish view, since it raises disturbing charges about Israel's

treatment of the Palestinians. Many in the west automatically give Israel a presumption of innocence. Evangelical Christians, who believe that all Jews should trust Jesus as Messiah, often argue that criticism of Israel is against God's will.

The case for Israel must not be based in the kind of zealous ideology that shows no regard for facts or openness to evidence. We must examine charges against Israel one by one, simply out of a concern for truth and justice. If

Declaration of the State of Israel May 14, 1948

Accordingly we, members of the People's Council, representatives of the Jewish community of Eretz-Israel and of the Zionist movement, are here assembled on the day of the termination of the British Mandate over Eretz-Israel and, by virtue of our natural and historic right and on the strength of the resolution of the United Nations General Assembly, hereby declare the establishment of a Jewish State in Eretz-Israel, to be known as the State of Israel.

THE STATE OF ISRAEL will be open for Jewish immigration and for the Ingathering of the Exiles; it will foster the development of the country for the benefit of all its inhabitants; it will be based on freedom, justice and peace as envisaged by the prophets of Israel; it will ensure complete equality of social and political rights to all its inhabitants irrespective of religion, race or sex; it will guarantee freedom of religion, conscience, language, education and culture; it will safeguard the Holy Places of all religions; and it will be faithful to the principles of the Charter of the United Nations.

Israel's policy about Palestine is fundamentally right, it will not crumble with this or that admission of fault, unless of course the evidence of Israeli guilt becomes overwhelming.

In the last fifteen years, the case for a Palestinian state has grown more popular among moderate Jews and many observers who are very sympathetic to Israel. Hans Küng, the great Christian theologian of Germany, wrote after the Gulf War in *Judaism: Between Yesterday and Tomorrow:* "The devastating consequences of the policy of occupation, including the moral consequences, are becoming increasingly clear to many Israelis. And as one who has so openly attacked the silence of Pius XII and the German bishops over the Jewish question, I may not keep silent over what Israelis are doing over the Palestinian question."

Küng's concerns have been echoed by Jewish writers. Amos Oz wrote in an editorial for *The New York Times:* "With or without Islamic fundamentalism, with or without Arab terrorism, there is no justification whatsoever for the lasting occupation and suppression of the Palestinian people by Israel. We have no right to deny Palestinians their natural right to self-determination."

He continues: "Two huge oceans could not shelter America from terrorism; the occupation of the West Bank and Gaza by Israel has not made Israel secure—on the contrary, it makes our self-defense much harder and more complicated. The sooner this occupation ends, the better it will be for Palestinians and Israelis alike."

The same point has been made most powerfully by Michael Lerner, the editor of *Tikkun* magazine, and one of America's leading liberal Jewish activists. Lerner has received numerous death threats for his advocacy of a

Palestinian state. However, his defense of the right of Palestinians to a homeland is in the context of strong denunciation of their terrorist attacks on Israel and the need for Palestinians to renounce their hatred of Jews.

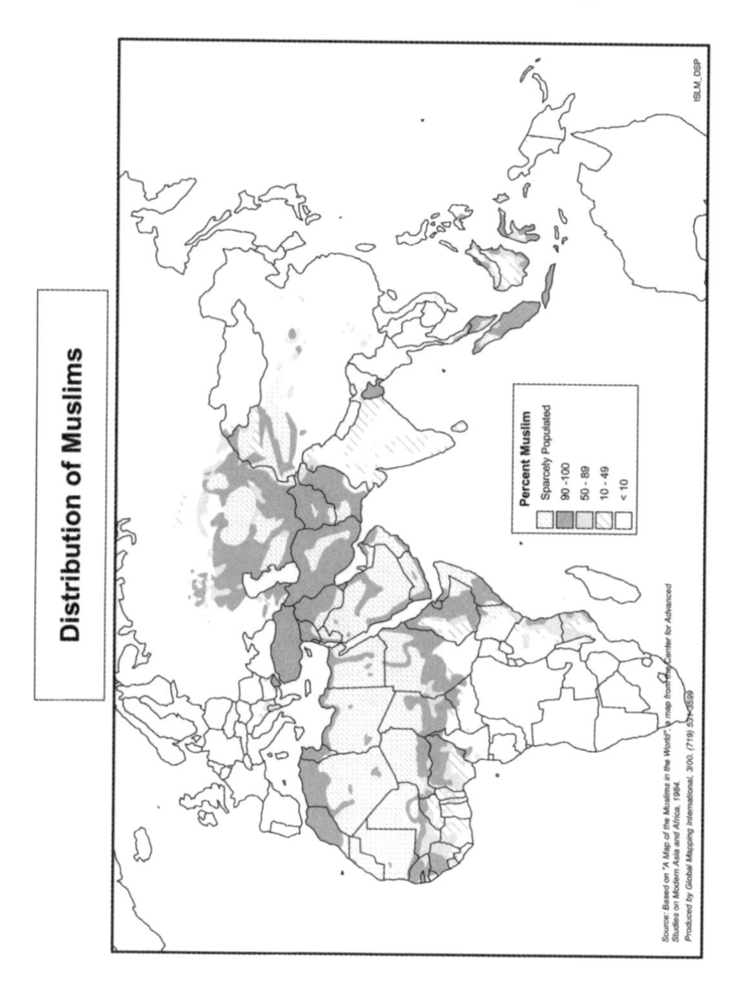

CHAPTER EIGHT

Now What?

It appears likely that all future attempts to understand Islam will be made in relation to September 11. That day is now marked in history in the same way as November 22, the day President John Kennedy died, and December 7, the attack on Pearl Harbor. In many ways it represents a turning point in the affairs of humanity.

Where we go from here depends on how the world responds to the events of that fateful day. As with any traumatic experience, September 11 can be the spark that ignites even greater tragedy, or it can stir all mankind to consciously turn from hatred and terror toward international understanding and peace.

How will Islam respond? Already we have seen hints in both directions. Muslim scholars have condemned the terrorist distortion of Islam, and people around the world—including Islamic nations—have expressed their sympathy and support for the victims of September 11. At the same time, militant Muslim demonstrations in several countries and continued terrorist attacks in Israel and elsewhere point the world toward chaos.

As noted earlier, there are two very different kinds of Islam. One group admires, defends, and supports the work of international terrorism in the name of Allah. The other, much larger group sees the actions of September 11 as a betrayal of Islam, the Prophet, and the Quran. Only time will reveal which view will carry the day.

President Bush made the distinction clear in his address to the joint session of Congress: "I also want to speak tonight directly to Muslims throughout the world. We respect your faith. It's practiced freely by many millions of Americans, and by millions more in countries that America counts as friends. Its teachings are good and peaceful, and those who commit evil in the name of Allah blaspheme the name of Allah. The terrorists are traitors to their own faith, trying, in effect, to hijack Islam itself. The enemy of America is not our many Muslim friends; it is not our many Arab friends. Our enemy is a radical network of terrorists, and every government that supports them."

As with all acts of evil, the events of September 11 force humanity to decide about the paths ahead, and which ones to choose. It is not inevitable that the evils of that day have to lead to other evils, or be the opening salvo into greater and greater cycles of terror. Humans, individually and collectively, can choose paths of goodness and peace because we have seen evil and do not want to go there anymore.

The peace that could emerge from Ground Zero will be hard to reach, since the enemies of love are so powerful, and hate is so deep in those who know nothing but terror's awful pull, especially a terror disguised in the name of God. The path to global peace demands the engagement of all people of good will. This cause must unite our planet, whether we are religious, atheist, or agnostic. September 11 demands a renewed determination to love justice, goodness, and peace so much that earth becomes a safer, more harmonious place.

The events of that terrible day demand a striving for real peace among all religious people of good will. September

11 was an act of evil carried out in the name of religion. It must be met by a billion acts of goodness by religious people. This is not to suggest that all religions are the same, but that religious people share common values.

What is needed is what Hans Küng has argued at the two most recent Parliaments of the World Religions: there will be no peace until there is peace between religions. He is not advocating some cheap agreement between faiths or endless theological debates. Rather, we must seek a deep, worldwide commitment to the paths of goodness that are taught by Christianity, Islam, and all major religions. When we stand on Ground Zero, shoulder to shoulder against the forces of terror, we are standing on common ground.

Since September 11, there have been endless editorials about the true nature of Islam. The divide has been predictable, but one that is important and necessary: yes, Osama bin Laden and the Taliban are true Muslims and they show us what Islam is really like; or, no, Islam is a religion of peace and bin Laden and the Taliban extremists are really a product of a militant fascism that has nothing to do with Muhammad or the Quran.

Quite possibly, in the days and years ahead Islam will redefine itself along new fault lines, as Muslims everywhere wrestle with new tensions, divided loyalties, and complex choices about what it means to practice Islam in a world scrutinizing every move made in the name of Allah.

Percent Muslim by Country

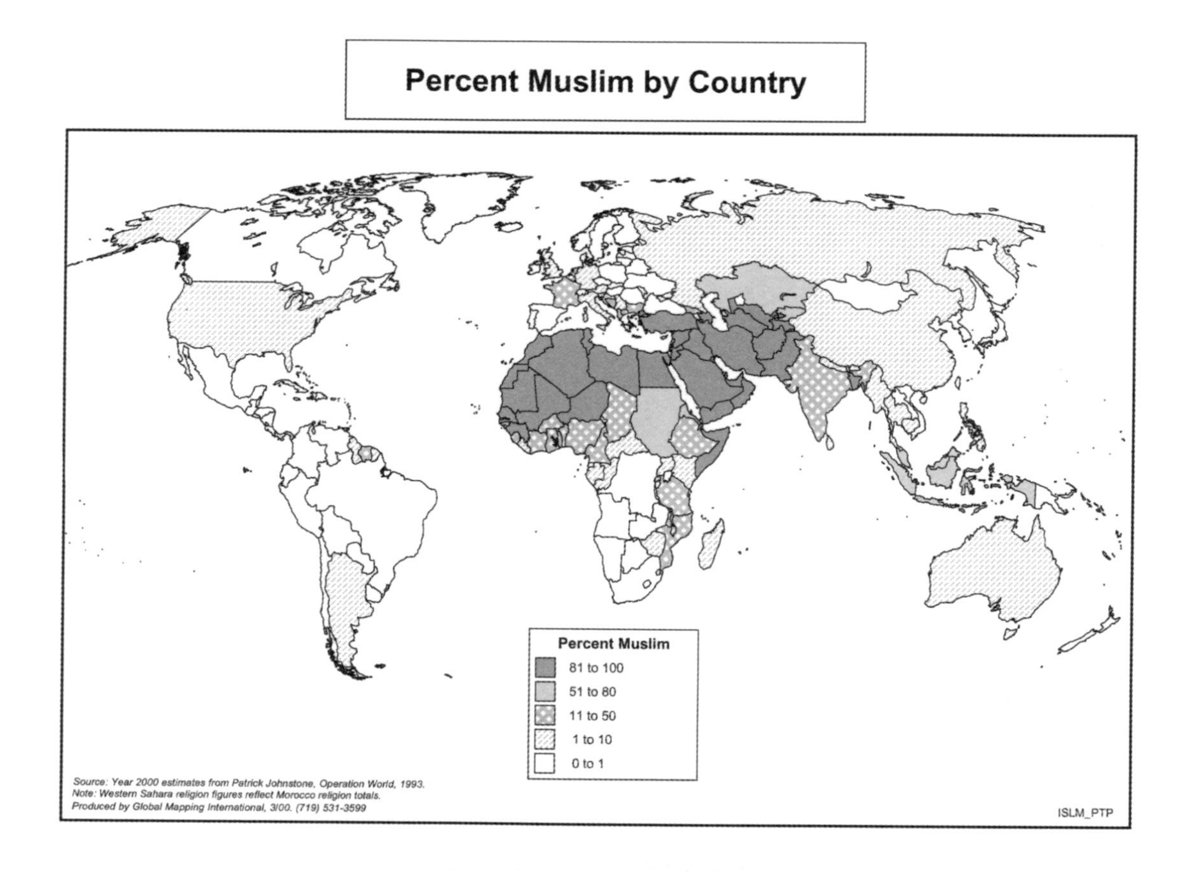

Glossary

A.H.—After *Hijrah* (the expulsion of Muhammad to Medina in A.D. 622), starting point in Muslim calendar

Allahu Akbar—means "God is the greatest"; used in Islamic prayers

Alim—a scholar or expert in Islam

Assalamu alaikum—Muslim greeting: "Peace be upon you"

Ayah (pl. ayat)—1. miracle or sign from God 2. Each verse of the Quran

Ayatollah—highest ranking religious leaders in Shia branch of Islam

Bismillahir rahmanir—phrase from the Quran which means "In the name of Allah, the Most Beneficent, the Most Merciful."

Barakallah—means "May the blessing of Allah be upon you"

Caliph or Khalifah—refers both to Muhammad's successors and to leaders of Islam in general

Dar ar-harb—Abode of war—territory outside Islamic control

Dar al-islam—Abode of Islam—territory under Islamic rule

Da'wah—mission of spreading Islam, evangelization

Dhimmi—non-Muslims living under Islamic control or law

Din—way of religion, way of life

Dunya—this life, this world

Du'a—a prayer

Eid—celebration or feast

Faqih—an expert or scholar in Islamic law or jurisprudence

Fard—anything that is obligatory, like praying five times per day

Fatihah—opening chapter of the Quran, recited in prayers

Fatwa—opinion or ruling in Islamic law

Fiqh—understanding and comprehension of Islamic law

Ghazi—term for soldier or warrior

Hadith—traditions about the prophet Muhammad

Hajj—the pilgrimmage to Mecca, one of the five pillars of Islam

Halal—something lawful or permitted, as in Halal food

Haraam—that which is illegal or not allowed in Islam

Haram—sanctuary or sacred territory, as in the haram of wives

Hijrah—refer to Muhammad's trip to Medina in A.D. 622 and is the first year of Islamic calendar (A.H.)

Iblis—Quranic word for Satan

Ijma—consensus in Islamic legal opinion

Imam—1. refers to spiritual or community leader in Islam 2. The person who leads prayer 3. In Shia Islam it refers to one of the early special leaders after Muhammad's death

Iman—trust, faith in Allah

Injil—the revelations given to the prophet Jesus (who is called Isa in Islam)

In sha' allah—means "If Allah wills" or "If Allah permits"

Isa—Jesus

Istighfar—to ask for divine forgiveness

Jihad—1. to strive, to endeavor 2. To engage in just war to defend Islam

Jinn—invisible spirit beings created by Allah, who can do good and bad just like humans

Jahannam—hell

Jahiliyyah—the state of ignorance and disobedience in Arabia before the Prophet arrived to give truth

Jizyah—the tax paid by non-Muslims in an Islamic country

Jannah—paradise, heaven

Kabah or Kaba—shrine or house of worship in the great mosque of Mecca, that Muslims believe was built by Abraham

Kafir—an unbeliever, someone who rejects Allah and his way

Kalam—Islamic logic and philosophy; can also mean speech

Khutbah—sermon or speech, used of sermon at Friday prayers

Laat—a major goddess figure in pre-Islamic Arabia

La ilaha illallah—means "There is no God but Allah"—first part of confession of faith necessary to be a Muslim

Mahdi—a term in various divisions of Shia Islam for either the seventh or twelfth ruler who went into a state of hiding and is expected back at the end of time

Masjid—house of worship (mosque in English)

Miraj—when Muhammad was taken to heaven by the angel Gabriel

Mufti—an expert in Muslim law

Mujahid—a fighter for Islam (both literally and figuratively)

Mushrik—someone who believes in more than one God

Munafiq—a hypocrite or deceiver

Nabi—a prophet or messenger from God

P.B.U.H.—abbreviation for Peace Be Upon Him, said after reference is made to Muhammad

Qiblah—direction Muslims face when they pray to Mecca

Quraysh—Muhammad's tribe, the most powerful in Arabia

Ramadan—month in Muslim calendar when revelations were first given to Muhammad and month when Muslims fast

Rasul—messenger or prophet

Salah—pillar of special communion or prayer five times per day

Sawm—pillar of total fasting during Ramadan

Shahadah—first pillar of confession: "There is no God but Allah, and Muhammad is His prophet."

Shaikh (or Sheikh)—religious leader or wise person in Islam, also elderly person

Shari'ah—the rules or laws of Islam

Shirk—the most serious offense of idol worship, teaching that God has partners, or putting something ahead of Allah

Sunnah—the life and deeds or way of Muhammad

Surah (pl. suwar)—refers to the chapter divisions of the Quran

S.A.W.—abbreviation of "Salla Allahu 'Alaihi Wa Sallam" which means "May the Blessing of Allah be upon Him" and is to be said or written when reference is made to Muhammad

Taqwa—the reverence or fear of Allah which leads to obedience

Tawaf—ritual of going around the Kabah seven times during pilgrimmage to Mecca

Ummah—the community of believers in Allah

Uzzah—major goddess worshiped in pre-Islamic Arabia

Wudu—washing or purification that is to take place before prayers

Zakat (or Zakah)—the pillar of giving a percent of wealth for the needy

FAQs

(Frequently Asked Questions)

1. Is the Quran the same as the Koran?

Yes. Koran is the older English word that is now obsolete among scholars. To be absolutely technical the best English rendering is Qur'an.

2. Is Mohammed the same as Muhammad?

Yes. These are simply two different English spellings for the Arabic word for Muhammad but they refer to the same person.

3. Do Muslims like to be called Muhammadans?

No. They really dislike the term since they claim to be followers of Allah, not Muhammad. Though they hold Muhammad in the highest regard, he is not divine.

4. Can the Quran be understood in English?

Yes, though even in Arabic the Quran is not written in a very orderly manner. The English translations lose the beauty of the Arabic, but they are faithful to the original language, especially the translation by A. J. Arberry.

5. Is Islam a religion of the sword?

Yes, to some degree. Muhammad engaged in military battles against his enemies and Muslim leaders created a vast empire through war. However, while Muslims believe in just war, the Quran forbids using force to convert people.

6. Did Muhammad really believe what he taught?

Yes. Critics of Muhammad who argue that he was a fraud pay little attention to the enormous evidence of his total commitment to his religion. He actually fought in military battle to defend his faith, something hard to imagine if he was a con artist.

7. Do Muslims have anything comparable to the Christian conversion experience?

Yes, in a sense. Islam teaches that everyone is born a Muslim by being a creation of Allah. Conversion to Islam is explained as reversion back to the original faith of their birth. Some who revert to Islam have very dramatic conversion stories.

8. Do Muslims believe they can go to heaven if they do not make the pilgrimage to Mecca?

All Muslims must make the pilgrimage if health and finances permit. To refuse to go to Mecca is a very grave and serious offense against Allah's law.

9. When Muslims pray, do they just recite phrases they have been taught, or do they pray from the heart?

Prayers by Muslims are often recited, as during the five prayer times each day, but Muslims also pray to Allah at other times in their own words. All prayers must be from the heart.

10. Is it true that only men go to the mosque for worship?

No. Men are expected to go to the mosque but women are allowed, although they pray in separate areas from men, for reasons of modesty and purity.

11. When Muslims pray five times each day, how long is each prayer time?

The length varies during each of the five prayer times, but one can count on praying at least one hour every day.

12. What do Muslims do if they are traveling—in a car or airplane—at a time for prayer?

There are complex rules about how Muslims are to pray during travel. It depends on who they are with, what prayer time is involved, and whether travel can be interrupted.

13. Where and when do women worship?

Women are to pray five days per day, just like men. They usually worship at home.

14. Women in traditional Muslim countries are often fully veiled in public. Why are Muslim women in the U.S. usually not veiled that way?

Veiling customs vary in Muslim countries and also in the United States. There are some American Muslim groups that demand total veiling, but most Muslim women in the United States have adopted a more relaxed public dress code based on the Islamic teaching they follow.

15. Are non-Arab Muslims considered second-class citizens in Islam?

Though Islam teaches that all Muslims are equal, non-Arab Muslims are sometimes treated as second-class citizens in Saudi Arabia or other parts of the Middle East.

16. Do Muslims say grace before meals?

Muslims are to thank Allah for food and drink both before and after meals.

17. Is there a specific age at which boys begin to participate at the mosque?

No, this varies, but Muslim leaders encourage parents to teach their children the daily prayers as early as the age of two.

18. Does the imam perform the same functions as a Christian pastor?

Generally, the Muslim imam performs the same functions as the Christian pastor: teaching, leading in prayer, counseling, and giving advice. The imam's role differs mainly in helping Muslims to apply the details of Islamic law.

19. In what areas of the world is Islam growing today?

Islam is growing rapidly in the United States, especially among Blacks, and in Southern Europe. Throughout the twentieth century Islam grew significantly in the sub-Saharan areas of Africa.

20. What is the biggest challenge facing Islam today?

The leaders of Islam must address the issue of personal freedom under Islamic rule. As well, Muslims must now decide what response they will make to militant, extremist versions of the faith.

Bibliography and Resources

General

George W. Braswell, Jr., *Islam* (Nashville: Broadman & Holman, 1996).

Hans Küng, *Christianity and the World Religions* (New York: Doubleday, 1986).

Bernard Lewis, *Islam and the West* (New York: Oxford, 1993).

Paul Marshall, ed., *Religious Freedom in the World* (Nashville: Broadman & Holman, 2000).

Fazlur Rahman, *Islam* (Chicago: University of Chicago Press, 1979).

Andrew Rippin, *Muslims* (London: Rutledge, 2000).

Ibn Warvaq, *Why I Am Not a Muslim* (Amherst: Prometheus, 1995).

Muhammad

Michael Cook, *Muhammad* (New York: Oxford, 1983).

F. E. Peters, *Muhammad and the Origins of Islam* (Albany: State University of New York Press, 1994).

William E. Phipps, *Muhammad and Jesus* (New York: Continuum, 1996).

W. Montgomery Watt, *Muhammad: Prophet and Statesman* (London: Oxford, 1961).

Muslims

Albert Hourani, *A History of the Arab Peoples* (Cambridge: Harvard, 1991).

V. S. Naipaul, *Among the Believers* (Harmondsworth: Penguin, 1982).

Seyyed Nasr, ed., *Islamic Spirituality: Manifestations* (London: SCM, 1991).

Women in Islam

Jan Goodwin, *Price of Honor* (New York: Little, Brown, & Co., 1994).

Fatima Mernissi, *The Veil and the Male Elite* (Boston: Addison-Wesley, 1991).

Jihad, Militant Islam, and Terrorism

John L. Esposito, *Islam and Politics* (Syracuse: Syracuse University Press, 1998).

Kanan Makiya, *Cruelty and Silence* (New York: W. W. Norton, 1993).

Judith Miller, *God Has Ninety-Nine Names* (New York: Simon & Schuster, 1996).

Israel and the Palestinian Question

Mitchell Bard, *Myths and Facts* (Chevy Chase, Md.: AICE, 2001).

David Grossman, *The Yellow Wind* (New York: Farrar Straus Giroux, 1988).

Thomas Friedman, *From Beirut to Jerusalem* (New York: Farrar Straus Giroux, 1989).

Michael Marrus, *The Holocaust in History* (Toronto: Lester & Orpen Dennys, 1987).

CD Resource

The World of Islam (Colorado Springs: Global Mapping International, 2001) See information on this CD at http://www.gmi.org.

Web Resources

The following web sites are recommended because of their intrinsic importance and the many links they provide to all aspects of the study of Islam.

http://answering-islam.org.uk
http://www.debate.org.uk

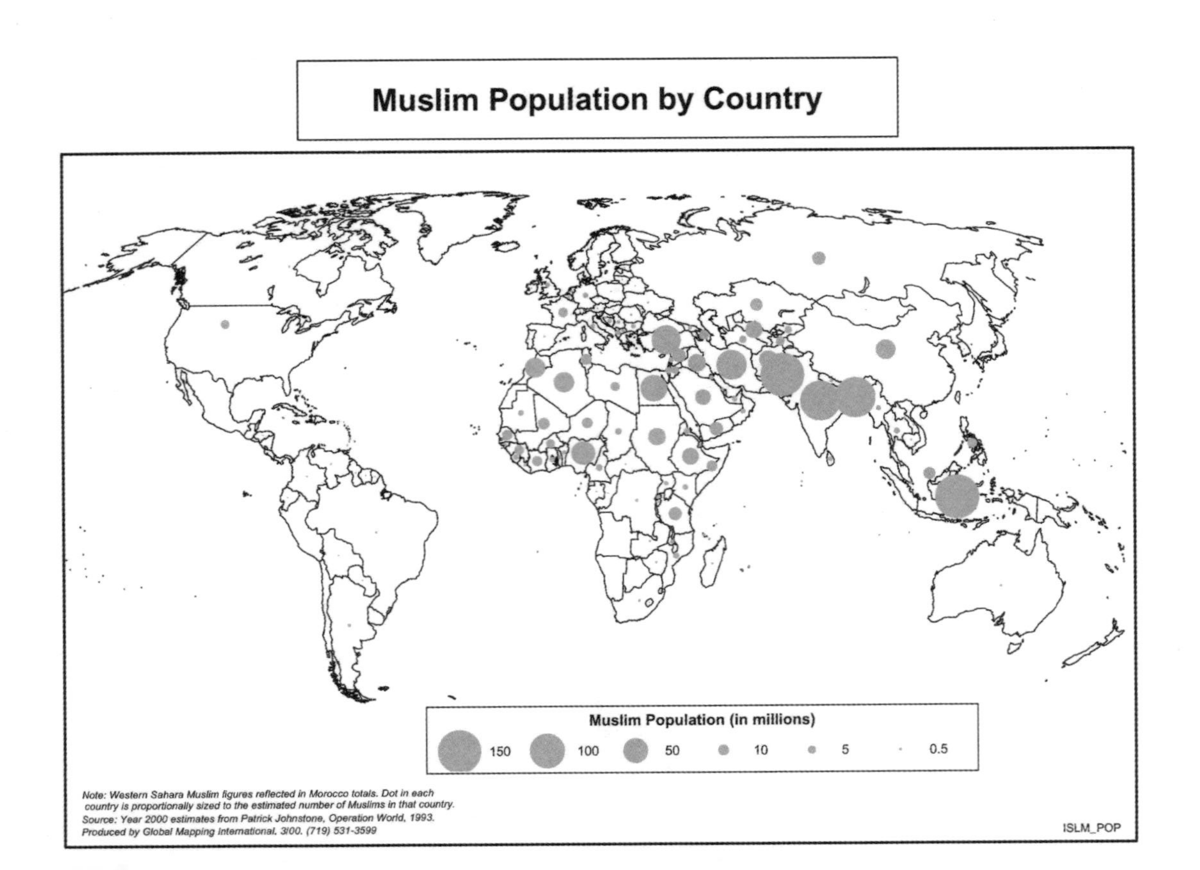
Muslim Population by Country
Muslim Population (in millions)
150
100
50
10
5
0.5
Note: Western Sahara Muslim figures reflected in Morocco totals. Dot in each country is proportionally sized to the estimated number of Muslims in that country.
Source: Year 2000 estimates from Patrick Johnstone, Operation World, 1993.
Produced by Global Mapping International. 3/00. (719) 531-3599
ISLM_POP